REV. ASA M[...] D.D.

BAPTISM
OF THE
Holy Spirit

✤

INCLUDES

GOD'S PROVISION
OF POWER

BY CHARLES G. FINNEY

WILLIAMS
PUBLISHERS

CLINTON, NEW YORK

THE BAPTISM OF THE HOLY SPIRIT/
GOD'S PROVISION OF POWER
Published by Williams Publishers
Republication of the 1880 edition
originally published by Elliot Stock, London
titled *The Baptism of the Holy Ghost/
The Enduement of Power*

Scripture is taken from *The Holy Bible,*
King James Version

Cover and interior design
by UDG |DesignWorks, Sisters, OR

ISBN 0-9718789-2-7

Williams Publishers' logo is a trademark
of Williams Publishers
3843 Fountain St.
Clinton, NY 13323

T: 315.853.4217
F: 315.853.1979
www.williamspublishers.com
info@williamspublishers.com

Printed in the United States of America
1 2 3 4 5 6 7 8 9 - 08 07 06 05 04 03 02

Contents

Preface . . . . *v*

THE BAPTISM OF THE HOLY SPIRIT
by Asa Mahan

1. Introduction—The Christian Character, and How to Attain it . . . 13

2. Experience and Teachings of our Saviour on
   the Baptism of the Holy Ghost 23

3. Doctrine of the Baptism of the Holy Ghost
   Explained and Elucidated 35

4. Baptisms of the Spirit Under the Old and New
   Dispensations Compared 51

5. Baptism of the Spirit Under the New Dispensation 63

6. The Preparation for the Baptism of the Spirit 79

7. Miscellaneous Suggestions in Regard to this Doctrine 93

8. The Fellowship of the Spirit 105

9. The Unity of the Spirit 117

10. Witness, Demonstration, and Power of the Spirit 127

11. The Fountain Opened for Sin and for Uncleanness, or
    The Cleansing Power of the Spirit 140

12. The Consolation of the Spirit, or
    The Uses of Afflictive Providences 155

God's Provision of Power
by Charles G. Finney

1. Reasons Why the Power is Not Received 173
2. An Exhibition of the Power From on High 177
3. Who May Expect this Enduement of Power 181
4. The Conditions of Receiving this Power 186

Preface

It is now quite six years since the following treatise has been before the American, and upwards of four since it has been before the English public. During this period it has been read by very many individuals on both sides of the Atlantic, and that, as the author has the best reasons for believing, with much affirmed interest and profit. During this period also the central theme of the treatise, "the Promise of the Spirit," "the Baptism of the Holy Ghost," the promised "Enduement of Power from on High," which became real in the experience of the apostles and their associates at the Pentecost, and had never been vouchsafed to the Church in such forms before, has become throughout Christendom a subject of thought, inquiry, prayer, and waiting expectation, unknown in centuries past. That this treatise has contributed something to bring about this desirable and most propitious and hopeful consummation, is not a matter of doubt. That it may hereafter continue to exert an important influence to prepare the way for the approaching "brightness of the Divine rising," is still an object of hope.

The special doctrine of the treatise takes specific form from the following declaration of our Saviour to His disciples:—"If ye love Me, keep My commandments. And I will pray the Father, and He shall give you another Comforter, that He may abide with you forever; even the Spirit of truth; whom the world cannot receive, because it seeth Him not, neither knoweth Him: but ye know Him; for He dwelleth with you, and shall be in you." The Holy Spirit had convinced these disciples of sin, had induced them to believe in Christ, to love Him, and to "keep His commandments." From the hour of their conversion He had been with them, and their bodies had been His temples. During the ten days in which those disciples "tarried in Jerusalem," waiting "the promise of the Father," the same Spirit was with them still, perfecting their obedience, intensifying their aspirations, unifying their "accord," and completing their preparation for the inward enlightenments, "enduements of power," Divine fellowships and fruitions, which were to result from the approaching "baptism." All that preceded the Pentecost was preparatory to this baptism, but no part of it. The conversion and subsequent preparation were the work of the Spirit, just as much as the baptism, and the former was indispensable to the latter. Had the apostles continued in the preparatory stage of experience, or had they gone forth to their work prior to the reception of "the promise of the Spirit," they would have remained to the end of life as they had been before, "a feeble folk," and the world would never have felt their influence. Waiting, on the other hand, "the promise of the Father," and going forth, as Christ did, "under the power of the Spirit," they soon "turned the world upside down."

The same holds true of all believers, the least as well as the greatest, under the present Dispensation, the Dispensation of the Spirit. As with the apostles and their associates, so with every believer in Jesus. After inducing "repentance toward God, and faith toward our Lord Jesus Christ," the Spirit abides with and works in him, as He did in them prior to the Pentecost, and for the one purpose, to perfect his love and obedience and inward preparation, that "the Holy Ghost may fall on him as He did on them at the beginning." If the convert stops short of this great consummation, and if he does this especially under the belief that he did receive "the Baptism of the Holy Ghost" in conversion, and that, consequently, nothing remains for him but a gradual increase of what he then received, he will almost inevitably remain through life in the darkness and weakness of the old, instead of going forth to his life work under "the enduements of power," spiritual illuminations, transforming visions of the Divine glory, "fellowships with the Father and with His Son Jesus Christ," and "assurances of faith," "assurances of hope," and "assurances of understanding," peculiar to the New Dispensation.

Here this great doctrine is met by the counter one, that every newborn soul does receive the promised "Baptism of the Holy Ghost," and all accompanying enlightenments and "enduements of power," at the time of his conversion. In confirmation of this doctrine such passages are adduced as those which affirm that the bodies of all believers "are the temples of the Holy Ghost," "that all have been baptized into one body," and that "if any man have not the Spirit of Christ, he is none of His." All this, we teach, is true of every convert now, and has been true of every converted person since the fall. The Holy Ghost had given the disciples "repentance unto life," and "was with them" as a sanctifying presence, had made their bodies His temple, and had "baptized them into one body," prior to the Pentecost. They must have had "the Spirit of Christ, or they could not have been His." Yet, in the New Testament sense of the words, "the Holy Ghost was not given," and they were not "baptized with the Holy Ghost," until "the Pentecost had fully come." So of all converts in this dispensation. They "have the Spirit of Christ," "the Spirit is with them," and their bodies, as those of all the holy have ever been, are "His temple." This was true, and must have been true of all the converts in Samaria before Peter and John came there. Yet "the Holy Ghost had not fallen upon one of them." How any person can contemplate the revealed results of "the Baptism of the Holy Ghost," and then affirm, in the presence of palpable facts, that every such convert has received "the enduements of power" included in "the promise of the Spirit," is a mystery of mysteries to us.

But while all believers have been "baptized into one body," are we not also told that "there is one baptism?" If the believer was in his conversion, with all others, baptized "by one Spirit into one body," and may afterwards be "baptized with the Holy Ghost," is there not, it is asked, more than one "baptism of the Spirit?" If we are to infer from such language that there is one and only "one baptism," what shall we do with the argument of the Friends, that water baptism should be dispensed with? The apostle does not say that there is "one baptism" of the Spirit; but "one baptism." While he says this, he speaks in another place of "the Doctrine of Baptisms." While baptism in all its forms is "one," just as "he that planteth and he that watereth are one," that is, one in purpose, spirit, and aim, so baptism may, for aught that appears in such expressions, be as diverse in its forms as are the individualities employed in planting and watering the churches. As there is "one body with many members," and "one faith" in many forms, so there may be "one baptism" in many forms.

According to the doctrine under consideration, two blessings as simultaneously given to every convert at the moment when he believes—

the pardon of sin, and "the Baptism of the Holy Ghost," with all its attendant "enduements of power," and this is the doctrine which the apostles intended to teach, and did teach. If this were so, why did Peter and John pray for the converts in Samaria, that they might receive the Holy Ghost, and not that they might receive the forgiveness of their sins?

Are we anywhere told in the New Testament that any have "received the Word of the Lord," believed in Jesus, openly confessed His name, and yet have not received the pardon of their sins? We do read of numbers, however, who thus believed, not one of whom had received the Holy Ghost at the time of believing, or after they had believed.

Take another case. Paul did put this question to the twelve believers whom he met at Ephesus; namely, "Have ye received the Holy Ghost since ye believed?" or, as some render the original, "Did ye receive the Holy Ghost when ye believed?" Why did he put this, and not the other question equally pertinent, if this doctrine is true, in each case, to wit: "Have ye received the pardon of your sins since ye believed?" or, "Did ye receive the pardon of your sins when ye believed?" Had he held and taught the dogma that both blessings are always and at the same moment given the instant an individual believes, he would have been just as likely to have asked if one blessing had been received, as whether the other had been, and the inquiry would have been infinitely absurd in either case.

The case of these twelve disciples is entirely clear from the reply often made to the argument based upon the revealed fact, that the Baptism of the Holy Ghost was given to the Jews at the Pentecost, to the Samaritans, and to the Gentiles in the house of Cornelius, not at the moment of regeneration, but "after they had believed." This was necessary, it is said, to verify for Jews, Samaritans, and Gentiles, common rights and privileges in the Church of Christ. After this the Holy Ghost is never given in this form, but always in regeneration. The question of Paul (Acts 19:1-7) was put to these believers many years after the baptisms above referred to, and after the New Dispensation had been established; however, these individuals did receive the Holy Ghost, not only "after they had believed," but after they had, as believers, been baptized (Acts 19:5, 6). The case is too plain to require comments.

No, reader: the apostles rightly understood our Saviour, and so taught, to wit, that the condition of pardon is "repentance toward God, and faith toward our Lord Jesus Christ," and that the condition on which "He will baptize with the Holy Ghost" is "love and obedience," and "waiting the promise of the Father," after we have believed. Hence they taught that the Holy Ghost is given not with forgiveness, but to "those who obey God." In Ezek. 36:27 and 37, we are absolutely taught that Christ as the Mediator of the new covenant will "put His Spirit within" believers; that is, "baptize them with the Holy Ghost," "when He shall be inquired of by them to do it for them." Language is without meaning, if "the promise of the Spirit" does not await the believer after he has entered into a state of justification, and then in a state of "love and obedience," and supreme consecration to Christ, "tarries" before God until he is "endued with power from on high." Having carefully weighed the contents of this introduction, the reader will be fully prepared to enter into the interior of the work itself.

The Baptism of the Holy Spirit

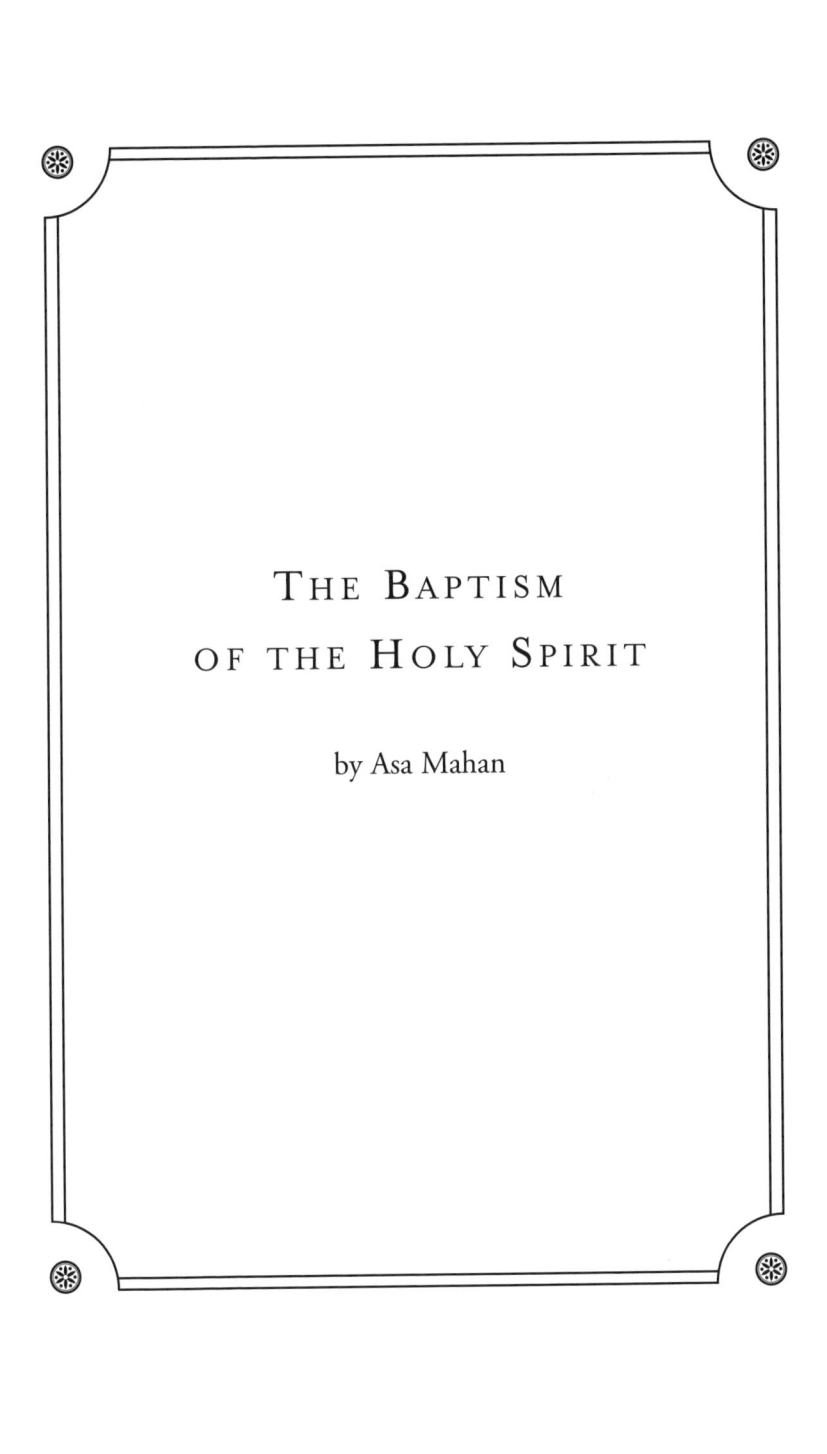

by Asa Mahan

Chapter 1

Introduction— The Christian Character and How to Attain It

❋

In the last day, that great day of the feast, Jesus stood and cried, saying, If any man thirst, let him come unto me, and drink. He that believeth on me, as the Scripture hath said, out of his belly shall flow rivers of living water. (But this spake He of the Spirit, which they that believe on Him should receive: for the Holy Ghost was not yet given; because that Jesus was not yet glorified.) —John 7:37–39

What shall we say then? That the Gentiles, which followed not after righteousness, have attained to righteousness, even the righteousness which is of faith. But Israel, which followed after the law of righteousness, hath not attained to the law of righteousness. Wherefore? Because they sought it not by faith, but as it were by the works of the law. For they stumbled at that stumbling stone. —Rom. 9:30–32

When Moses was about to build the Tabernacle, he received from God a solemn and specific admonition to "*make all things according to the pattern shown him in the Mount.*" We are Divinely taught and admonished in this requirement that when we attempt to accomplish any specific work which God has assigned us, we must, if we would not have the work fail in its accomplishment, strictly conform to God's revealed *pattern* and *method* of operation.

In the Scriptures there is very distinctly revealed a Divinely-developed and perfected pattern or model of Christian character, to which every believer is required to conform. God has also therein disclosed, with equal distinctness, the *method* by which that Christian character may be acquired, and take on the prescribed forms of beauty and perfection. This character is represented by the words "new man," as opposed to "the old man," our previous unrenewed moral and spiritual nature. The latter we are required to "put off," and the former to "take on." If we have failed to realize in our Christian character and experience *all* that is represented by the words, "new man in Christ Jesus," it must be for one of two reasons, or for both united. Either we have not *attempted* obedience to the command before us, or we have attempted in ways not conformable to His revealed *method*.

Two inquiries of vital importance here present themselves, viz., What is this "new man in Christ Jesus?" and, What is the revealed method by which we may "put off the old," and "put on the new man?" To each of these questions we will now proceed to give a concise and specific answer.

GOD'S IDEAL OF A CHRISTIAN

In Old Testament prophecy we have a very distinct revelation of God's ideal of the New Testament saint. He is a redeemed sinner who, under the provisions and influences of "the new covenant," has been Divinely cleansed "from all filthiness and from all his idols," and whose "iniquities shall be sought for, and there shall be none; and his sins, and they shall not be found." In "his feebleness he is as David," and in his strength "as the Lord, as the angel of the Lord before Him." "The sun is no more his light by day, neither for brightness does the moon give light unto him; but the Lord is unto him an everlasting light, and his God his glory. His sun does no more go down, neither does his moon withdraw itself: for the Lord is his everlasting light, and the days of his mourning are ended." In his experience has been realized, and is being realized, all that was spoken of by the prophet Joel: "And it shall come to pass in the last days, saith God, I will pour out of My Spirit upon all flesh; and your sons and your daughters shall prophesy, and your young men shall see visions, and your old men shall dream dreams; and on My servants and on My handmaidens I will pour out in those days of My Spirit; and they shall prophesy."

In the New Testament this "new man" is revealed as "after God created in righteousness and true holiness," and as "renewed in knowledge after the image of Him that created him;" as "beholding with open face the glory of the Lord, and being changed into the same image from glory to glory;" "as comprehending the breadth, and length, and depth, and height, and knowing the love of Christ, which passeth knowledge, and being filled with all the fullness of God;" as "walking in the light, as God is in the light;" as "having been made perfect in love;" and as "having fellowship with the Father, and with His Son Jesus Christ."

To him "Christ manifests Himself," and is formed within him "the hope of glory." He is "crucified with Christ," and "by the cross is crucified to the world, and the world to him." "He is in the world as Christ was in the world," and "in the name of Christ asks and receives until his joy is full;" and "believing in Christ he rejoices with joy unspeakable and full of glory." "Out of his belly flow rivers of living water." "When weak, he is made strong," and "in tribulation, distress, persecution, famine, nakedness, peril, sword, death, and life," he is " more than conqueror, through Him that hath loved us."

In him "tribulation worketh patience; and patience experience; and experience hope;" and "all things work together for his good." When "troubled on every side, he is not distressed; when perplexed, he is not in despair; when persecuted, he is not forsaken; and when cast down, he is not destroyed." In every condition of existence he finds deep content in the center of the sweet will of God, and verifies in experience the great central fact of the Divine life—that "we can do all things through Christ who strengtheneth us."

Clad in the panoply of God, "he stands in the evil day," and "quenches all the fiery darts of the wicked." "His faith groweth exceedingly," and his "charity aboundeth;" and he is constantly growing "into the stature of the fulness of Christ." He also "has power with God and with men." "He asks what he will, and it is done unto him." As reflecting the image and glory of Christ, he is "the light of the world" and the "salt of the earth." Such is God's revealed pattern of the New Testament saint, "the new man" whom we are required to "put on."

HOW TO ATTAIN THIS CHARACTER

No one will question the correctness of the above presentation of God's revealed pattern of the New Testament saint, or affirm that we have given any unauthorized coloring to that representation. How shall we obey the command requiring us to "put off the old," and to "put on the new man?" Have we a revealed *method* of attaining this character? In answer to such inquiries, we remark:—

1. That whenever any of the leading characteristics of "the new man" are referred to in the Bible, they are specifically represented as produced by the *indwelling presence, special agency, and influence of the Holy Spirit.* Do we "behold with open face the glory of the Lord?" and are we thereby "changed into the same image?" It is "by the Spirit of the Lord;" and this "*liberty,*" this *cloudless sunlight,* we are expressly taught, is enjoyed where, and only "where the Spirit of the Lord is." Do we "have fellowship with the Father and with His Son Jesus Christ?" Does God "dwell in us and walk in us?" and do Christ and the Father "come to us" and "make their abode in us?" All this, we are expressly taught, is the "fellowship of the Spirit;" the fellowship which the Spirit induces and sustains.

Do we enjoy "assurance of hope?" It is because "the Spirit testifies to our spirit that we are the children of God." *Have we power in prayer? It is because "the Spirit maketh intercession for the saints, according to the will of God."* Do we call Jesus Lord? It is by the Holy Ghost. Have we no condemnation? It is because we are in Christ Jesus, and walk not after the flesh, but after the Spirit. Do we bear love, joy, peace? &c. They are said to be "the fruit of the Spirit."

Do we "mortify the deeds of the body?" It is "through the Spirit." Do we "comprehend the breadth, and depth, and length, and height, and know the love of Christ which passeth knowledge?" It is because we have been previously "strengthened with might by the Spirit in the inner man." Does Christ become to us "wisdom, righteousness, sanctification, and redemption?" It is because He is made such to us "of God;" that is, by the Spirit of God—the Spirit "revealing Christ in us," and showing us His grace and glory.

When Christ promises to every believer that "out of his belly shall flow rivers of living water," we must bear in mind that "this He spake of the Spirit." If, then, we would "put off the old man with his deeds," and "put on the new man, who after God is created in righteousness and true holiness," it must be through the prior indwelling of the Spirit in our hearts. On no other condition can we, in full conformity to God's revealed pattern, become New Testament saints.

2. This indwelling presence of the Spirit in our hearts, through which all these revelations of the Divine grace and glory occur, and all these moral and spiritual transformations are effected; through which all these Divine fellowships are possessed, and these assurances, "everlasting consolations and good hope, through grace," and this fulness of joy, are vouchsafed—this indwelling presence of the Spirit in our hearts, we say, is given to us AFTER we have, through His convicting power, "repented of sin, and believed in Christ."

Nothing is or can be more plain than the teachings of inspiration on this subject. "Faith cometh by hearing;" "the sealing and earnest of the Spirit" are received "*after* we have believed." When Christ "spoke of the Spirit," He spoke of a blessing which "they that believe were *afterward* to receive." The Spirit "convinces the world of sin, of righteousness, and of judgment," and thus induces "repentance toward God, and faith toward our Lord Jesus Christ," but He "comes upon," "falls upon," or "endues with power from on high" only such as have already believed.

The inquiry which inspired apostles put to those who were believers was this: "Have ye received the Holy Ghost *since* ye believed?"

As soon as individuals were recognized as real believers in the Lord Jesus, special prayer was offered for them that "they might receive the Holy Ghost." No believer can fully realize in experience God's revealed pattern of the Christian character until he is "endued with power from on high." Then, and not till then, will he comprehend the height, and depth, and length, and breadth of Divine love, and be "filled with all the fulness of God."

3. The indwelling presence and power of the Spirit are to be sought and received by faith in God's word of promise, on the part of the believer, *after* he has believed; just as pardon and eternal life are to be sought by the sinner before justification. "How much more shall your heavenly

Father give the Holy Spirit to them that ask Him." Between the believer and the baptism of the Spirit lies "the promise of the Father." If this promise is not embraced by faith, the gift will not be vouchsafed.

Hence the apostles, as soon as a sinner was converted, and became a believer in Christ, turned and fixed his eye upon "the promise of the Spirit" as the crowning blessing of Divine grace, as the blessing without which he could not witness with power for the Lord Jesus.

Before Christ would allow His disciples to enter upon their world mission, He commanded them to "tarry in Jerusalem, until they were endued with power from on high." So He requires every believer, before he enters upon his life-work as a Christian, to tarry before God, and pray and wait, and wait and pray, until "the Holy Ghost shall fall upon him," as "He did upon the disciples at the beginning."

Here, then, we have God's revealed method of attaining this ideal of the Christian character—that is, of rendering real, in our experience and life, His Divinely-developed and perfected pattern of the New Testament saint. If, in our endeavors to render that model real in our experience, we "make all things according to the pattern shown us in the Mount," and if those endeavors accord with God's inspired plan, our characters and lives will be constantly taking on new and higher forms of radiant beauty and perfection. If, on the other hand, we fail to put forth the necessary endeavors, or if those endeavors shall take a wrong direction, God will utterly reject us as "reprobate silver;" or our spiritual lives will manifest a feeble and sickly growth, and when we should be risen "into the measure of the stature of the fulness of Christ," we shall be as "babes in Christ."

A FAILURE IN THE SPIRITUAL LIFE

"My life is a complete failure," said a very aged man, and the most wealthy that had then lived in the American nation. This term "failure" represents one of the most affectingly melancholy ideas that ever entered human mind. Life may be a failure for various reasons. No effective endeavors may be put forth in any direction. A purposeless, dreamy, effortless life is, of course, a dead failure.

A life full of purpose and activity may be a failure, because its *direction* has been towards worthless or unworthy ends. The ends and aims of the Christian life are the most worthy and important known, even to the infinite and eternal mind. To fail here, is to render existence itself a failure; and we do fail so far as we come short of our *available* privileges and advantages.

Not a few fail *totally,* because their so-called religious life is void of holy purpose, aim, and activity. Others, with the Jew, "follow after the law of righteousness," without "attaining to the law of righteousness," and that because their activity is self-originated, and void of faith as its central principle. Others still have in reality holy purposes and aims, and their lives take on some forms of real Christian activity. They have, also, a form of saving faith. Their lives, however, are comparative failures, because they live far below their privileges, and never possess or exercise "the power with God and with men," which is Divinely offered them to possess and exercise.

Let us for a moment turn our attention to the twelve disciples whom Paul met at Ephesus—who had believed, but not "received the Holy Ghost since they believed." Suppose that for want of better instruction they had continued till death in the same state in which they then were. They might have been saved at last; but their lives as Christians would have been melancholy failures as compared with what they were after "the Holy Ghost came upon them."

When Apollos first came to Ephesus he was "mighty in the Scriptures," was "instructed in the way of the Lord," was "fervent in spirit," and "taught diligently the way of the Lord." Like the twelve above referred to, however, "he knew only the baptism of John," and as a consequence "had not received the Holy Ghost since he believed." If no one had "expounded to him the way of God more perfectly," he would probably have continued as before. He might have been saved himself, and done *some* good: but his life would have been in many important respects a vast failure, as compared with what it did become after he was instructed in the "way of God more perfectly."

Christian reader, shall your life, in any form, be a failure? To prevent this, to "teach you the way of God more perfectly," if you do not yet know it, and to insure to you a life of which God shall not be ashamed, is the end for which this treatise has been prepared.

In no era of Church history, since the primitive age passed away, has the mission and "promise of the Spirit" occupied so much attention among all classes of believers as now. We regard this as a glorious sign of the times. We pray that the results of this attention may be a Pentecostal baptism of the Holy Ghost upon all churches throughout the Christian world.

There are two distinct forms of instruction upon this subject, which we briefly notice.

According to one, "the promise of the Spirit" as an indwelling Spirit is always fulfilled at the moment of conversion. What is subsequently to be expected is merely a continuation and gradual increase of what was then conferred.

According to the other view, the Spirit first of all induces in the sinner "repentance towards God and faith toward our Lord Jesus Christ." Then, "after he has believed," that is, after conversion, "the Holy Ghost comes upon," "falls upon," and is "poured out upon him," and thus "endues him with power from on high" for his life mission and work. In this baptism of power, this "sealing and earnest of the Spirit," "the promise of the Spirit" is fulfilled.

This is the view which we shall endeavor to sustain in this volume.

It seems undeniable that if this last is not the correct view, inspired men have fundamentally erred upon this subject. With them conversion was not *prima-facie* evidence that the convert had received "the sealing and earnest of the Spirit." Hence the question which they put to converts, viz., "Have ye received the Holy Ghost since ye believed?" The apostles did not deny or depreciate the importance or necessity of the Spirit's influences in conviction, conversion, and the whole work of justification. Nor would we by any means be supposed to entertain such an error. The Spirit is in the world to "convince of sin, of righteousness, and of judgment," to induce "repentance toward God, and faith toward our Lord Jesus Christ," and thus perfect the work of justification. Nor does the Spirit leave the convert when this necessary work is accomplished, but is ever present, preparing him for the promised baptism of Himself which is yet to be received by him.

Repentance and justification, and the Spirit's influences in producing the same, are necessary prerequisites for this great consummation. When the sacred writers employed such terms and phrases as the following: "The Holy Ghost was not yet given," "The Holy Ghost had not fallen upon any of them," "The promise of the Spirit," "The sealing and earnest of the Spirit," "Have ye received the Holy Ghost since ye believed?" and "Baptized with the Holy Ghost," they referred to the promised baptism of the Spirit, by which we are "endued with power from on high," "after we have believed." As "the promise of the Spirit" awaits the believer *after* conversion, the apostles did not regard the *fact* of conversion as certain *proof* that the convert had "received the Holy Ghost" in His baptismal power.

The fact stands recorded, that many individuals were truly converted in Samaria under the preaching of Philip, and that upon not one of them "had the Holy Ghost fallen" when Peter and John first appeared among them. There were many holy men and holy women among the followers of Christ prior to His crucifixion. The Holy Ghost, as promised in the New Testament, however, was not given, as we are positively informed, until *after* "Jesus was glorified." The New Testament saints were "sealed with the Holy Spirit of promise" "after they believed," and not when they were converted. This is sufficient for the present, as the whole subject will be fully elucidated in subsequent pages.

How many thousands there are in the churches who have been converted, but are yet without the baptism of the Holy Ghost! They have been baptized with water, and believed according to the use of that term; but ask their hearts and their lives, "Have ye received the Holy Ghost since ye believed?" Their doubts and fears, their lukewarmness and selfishness, their bigotry and worldliness, their errings and falls, give the answer.

Those who sustain the sacred relations of pastors and teachers have received a special commission to "feed the Church of God, which He hath purchased with His own blood." This commission is rendered specially sacred by the fact that of this flock "the Holy Ghost has made us overseers." When we come to this blood-bought flock, what direction shall our teachings take upon the subject under consideration? If there is any subject that we need to understand, it is this. If there is any subject on which we should borrow our light from "the sure word of prophecy," and on which our instructions should absolutely accord with that word, it is this. On no subject is wrong instruction more certain to render the religious life a failure.

If "the promise of the Spirit" is fulfilled in conversion, and we teach that "the baptism," "the sealing," and "the earnest of the Spirit" are to be sought and received "*after* we have believed," then we instruct believers to fix their hearts upon what they are never to find.

If, on the other hand, believers are to "receive the Holy Ghost" as promised, and are "endued with power from on high," not in conversion, but "*after* they have believed;" and we impress upon their minds the opposite view, then we impart a life-long misdirection to their seekings, prayers, and activities. We send them in the direction of darkness, instead of "marvelous light;" of weakness, instead of strength; of doubt, instead of "full assurance of hope;" of emptiness, instead of the "fulness of God;" and of the "bondage of corruption," instead of "the glorious liberty of the sons of God." Will you not attend us in a careful investigation of this great theme? If we go wrong, will you not expose the error? If we shall speak "the words of truth and soberness," will you not hold up the light before the Church of God?

Reader, the subject before us is not one of mere speculative interest. It is, on the other hand, one of vital importance relatively to the life of God in your soul. If, when you have read what we hope to write, you do not find yourself nearer to God than you now are; if you do not find yourself in full "fellowship with the Father and with His Son Jesus Christ," and if "your joy shall not be full," or you shall not be earnestly moved to "seek with all your heart and with all your soul" until you find this infinite good; then so far we have written, and you have read, in vain.

If you have not "received the Holy Ghost since you believed," you need to know *certainly* whether there is not in reserve for you "some better thing" than you have yet obtained. Will you not read these pages with the fixed purpose to know, if possible, the truth upon this whole subject, and, if you find the light, to follow it, until you are "filled with all the fulness of God?"

Chapter 2

Experience and Teachings of Our Saviour on the Baptism of the Holy Ghost

This Jesus hath God raised up, whereof we all are witnesses. Therefore being by the right hand of God exalted, and having received of the Father the promise of the Holy Ghost, He hath shed forth this, which ye now see and hear. —Acts 2:32–33

For He whom God hath sent speaketh the words of God; for God giveth not the Spirit by measure unto Him. —John 3:34

In Christ there were two forms of manifestation equally conspicuous—viz., Deity "in the brightness of His glory," and "the express image of His person;" and humanity in absolute beauty and perfection. In the former relation He is "the Lord our righteousness." In the latter, He is our Divine-human Exemplar, teaching us not only what we should do and become, but *how* to do and become all that is required of us.

Here arises a new question, which, to our knowledge, has not been put before. The question is this: Did the development or manifestation of the spiritual life in Christ depend upon the baptism, the indwelling, and the influence of the Holy Spirit, the same in all essential particulars as in us? Did He seek and secure this Divine anointing as the necessary conditions and means of "finishing the work which the Father had given Him to do"—just as we are necessitated to seek and secure the same "enduement of power from on high," as the means and condition of our finishing the work which Christ has given us to do?

A reference to prophecy furnishes a definite answer to all such questions: "And there shall come forth a rod out of the stem of Jesse, and a Branch shall grow out of his roots, and the Spirit of the Lord shall be upon Him, the spirit of wisdom and understanding, the spirit of counsel and might, the spirit of knowledge and the fear of the Lord; and shall *make* Him of quick understanding in the fear of the Lord." Isa. 11:1–3. Here we are positively taught that the Divine manifestations which shone through Christ were the result of the power of the Spirit which rested upon Him.

The same truth is taught in Isa. 42:1: "Behold My servant, whom I uphold! Mine elect, in whom My soul delighteth; I have put My Spirit upon Him; He shall bring forth judgment to the Gentiles." In Isa. 61:1, Christ thus speaks of Himself in the first person: "The Spirit of the Lord God is upon Me; because He hath anointed Me to preach good tidings unto the meek, He hath sent Me to bind up the heartbroken, to proclaim liberty to the captives, and the opening of the prison to them that are bound." The fact that Christ was thus baptized of the Spirit implies that He needed that baptism, and that without it, in the relations in which He then was, He could not have "finished the work which the Father had given Him to do." In seeking, and obtaining, and acting under that baptism, Christ is our Exemplar in respect to the spiritual and Divine life which is required of us.

We find the same truth set forth with equal clearness in the New Testament. In John 3:34, we are told, for example, that the reason why Christ spake *as* He did, and *what* He did, was owing to the measureless effusion and power of the Spirit which was vouchsafed to Him: "For He whom God hath sent speaketh the words of God; for God giveth not the Spirit by measure unto Him." God does not bestow gifts or influences where and when they are not needed. Christ received this measureless effusion of the Spirit at the beginning and during the progress of His mission, because it was a necessity to Him—just as similar baptisms are a necessity to us in our life mission.

We have here, no doubt, one reason for the fact, that our Saviour spent so much time alone with God and in prayer to Him. Christ teaches us that God gives the Holy Spirit to those who ask, and seek, and knock at the door of mercy for this anointing. In this respect, also, God has made Christ our Exemplar, giving the Spirit to Him when he consciously needed His special Divine influence and sought for it, just as He gives us the Spirit as we consciously need and seek Him at His hands.

Not to be misled here, we must carefully distinguish between the state of Christ when, as the eternal Word, He dwelt with the Father, and when, as the same Word, He "was made flesh and dwelt among us." In the former state, He had infinite all-sufficiency in Himself; in the latter, He "was in all respects made like unto His brethren," and had the same need of the baptism of the Spirit that we have, and obtained "power from high" on the conditions on which the same blessing is promised to us.

We now turn to the recorded facts of the public life of our Saviour which bear upon our present inquiries. At the time of His baptism by John, the Spirit descended upon Him in answer to special prayer on His part: "Jesus also being baptized, and praying, the heaven was opened, and the Holy Ghost descended in a bodily shape like a dove upon Him." This was His first special baptism.

At the close of the temptation in the wilderness, after Satan had fled discomfited from His presence, and angels had descended and ministered unto Him, the final and great baptism appears to have been given, and "Jesus returned in the power of the Spirit into Galilee." The power which attended His preaching under this special Divine influence is thus presented by the sacred historian: "And there went out a fame of Him through all the region round about. And He taught in their synagogues, being glorified of all." But the effect of this baptism is still more manifest in the account which follows of His visit to Nazareth. We give the account in full:

"And He came to Nazareth, where He had been brought up; and, as His custom was, He went into the synagogue on the Sabbath day, and stood up for to read. And there was delivered unto Him the book of the prophet Esaias. And when He had opened the book, He found the place where it was written, The Spirit of the Lord is upon Me, because He hath anointed Me to preach the gospel to the poor; He hath sent Me to heal the broken-hearted, to preach deliverance to the captives, and recovering of sight to the blind, to set at liberty them that are bruised, to preach the acceptable year of the Lord. And He closed the book, and gave it again to the minister, and sat down. And the eyes of all them that were in the synagogue were fastened on Him. And He began to say unto them, This day is this Scripture fulfilled in your ears. And all bare Him witness, and wondered at the gracious words which proceeded out of His mouth."

Our Saviour was here among the people, who had known Him from childhood up. Hitherto He took no part in their worship but what was ordinary. Nor does it seem that His prior reading or discourses had been marked by peculiarities which excited very special observation, much less the envy of any. But now there was a mysterious something even about His reading, which fixed the eyes of all present upon Him. But their surprise and wonder reached their consummation when they listened to "the gracious words which proceeded out of His mouth."

In His intellectual, moral, and spiritual manifestations He stood before them as completely transformed as He was physically to the eyes of the disciples on the Mount of Transfiguration. Now this wonderful transformation Christ attributes, in fact and form, to the baptism of the Spirit which He had just before received. One of the main objects of reading that passage unquestionably was to explain to that people the cause of that transformation—a transformation so great as to excite their envy. We are in no danger of being misunderstood here. The life and character of our Saviour, prior to that event, were as absolutely pure as now. He was no less then than now, "God manifest in the flesh." Yet He had, through that baptism of love, knowledge, and power, ascended from some forms of perfect human and perfect Divine manifestations, to others far higher and more impressive.

The great truth which we would impress upon all minds through this revealed fact is this: If Christ the pure and spotless One, Christ the Eternal Word, was thus transformed through the "baptism of the Holy Ghost," what must be the transformation in believers when they for their life work shall "be endued with power from on high." This is the transformation which Christ is ready to effect in all His people. "He shall baptize you," says John Baptist, "with the Holy Ghost." On another occasion, when

John saw Jesus coming unto him he gave utterance to these memorable words: "Behold the Lamb of God, which taketh away the sin of the world! This is He of whom I said, After me cometh a man which is preferred before me: for He was before me. And I knew Him not: but that He should be made manifest to Israel, therefore am I come baptizing with water. And John bare record, saying, I saw the Spirit descending from Heaven like a dove, and it abode upon Him, and I knew Him not: but He that sent me to baptize with water, the same said unto me: Upon whom thou shalt see the Spirit descending, and remaining on Him, the same is He which baptizeth with the Holy Ghost. And I saw, and bare record that this is the Son of God."

We, then, are to look to Christ for the gift of the Spirit, just as He looked to the Father for the same baptism of power. As Christ spent forty days and forty nights in fasting and prayer preparatory to the reception of a full and final baptism, we should not think it strange if a considerable time should pass before such preparation in us is consummated.

Let this truth, however, be continually in our minds. The power of the Spirit was a necessity even to Christ for the full accomplishment of His life mission. How much more so to us if we would accomplish our life work. Christ would not enter upon His mission until He could "go forth in the power of the Spirit." Would it not be presumption in us to enter upon ours without tarrying before God "until we be endued with power from on high?"

We have now arrived at the main object of the present chapter—viz., what Christ Himself said and taught in regard to the Holy Spirit and His mission. On this part of our subject we would present the following facts and considerations:—

1. He taught expressly that *all* believers may seek and obtain this unspeakable gift, and upon the same conditions on which He obtained it. In Luke 11:4–13, we have specific instructions on this subject. Read the whole passage: "And I say unto you, Ask, and it shall be given you; seek, and ye shall find; knock, and it shall be opened unto you. For everyone that asketh, receiveth; and he that seeketh, findeth; and to him that knocketh, it shall be opened. If a son ask bread of any of you that is a father, will he

give him a stone? or if he ask a fish, will he for a fish give him a serpent? or if he shall ask an egg will he offer him a scorpion? If ye, then, being evil, know how to give good gifts unto your children, how much more shall your heavenly Father give the Holy Spirit to them that ask Him!"

All, then, are without excuse who go forth to the mission of life without doing so under "the power of the Spirit," as Christ went out from the wilderness. The heart of God, only in greater strength, is towards us, in respect to this gift, as the parental heart is toward the child in respect to needed food: "How much more shall your heavenly Father give the Holy Spirit to them that ask Him!"

2. The Holy Spirit, when given and not subsequently grieved or quenched, remains with us, not as a mere Divine influence, but as an abiding *personal* presence. Everywhere our Saviour speaks of the Spirit, not as an influence, but as a Person. As a Person He is sent—comes, speaks, teaches, shows things to the mind, and abides with believers, as Christ "dwelt among us." He requires the ordinance of baptism to be administered in "the name of the Father, and of the Son, and of the Holy Ghost." No such language is applicable to mere influence in any form.

The Spirit, also, when He comes to us, comes to abide with us as a *permanent* personal presence. Christ "came forth from the Father," came into the world, and "dwelt among us" for a little season. Then He "left the world, and returned to the Father." The Spirit comes to the believer to "abide with him forever." As a consequence, "all our work should be wrought in God," and all our activities should be under His immediate control. "I will pray the Father for you, and He shall give you another Comforter, that He may abide with you forever." "Ye know Him, for He dwelleth with you, and shall be in you."

3. Another truth of great moment taught by our Saviour on this subject, is this:—The benefits which we may all receive through the Spirit dwelling in us are far greater than His disciples did derive, or could have derived, from Christ's personal presence, teachings, and influence, when He was upon earth, and Himself under "the power of the Spirit." This we could hardly believe but upon the express testimony of our Saviour Himself. Until after "Christ was glorified," the Holy Ghost could not be

given, even to believers. Hence the highest good of His disciples demanded that He should return to the Father, that the abiding presence of the Spirit might be vouchsafed to them: "Nevertheless, I tell you the truth; it is expedient for you that I go away; for if I go not away, the Comforter will not come unto you; but if I depart, I will send Him unto you." Christ did not undervalue the light and privileges enjoyed by His disciples under His ministrations. On this subject He thus speaks: "And He turned Him unto His disciples, and said privately, Blessed are the eyes which see the things that ye see; for I tell you that many prophets and kings have desired to see those things which ye see, and have not seen them; to hear those things which ye hear, and have not heard them." But what they thus saw and heard was only preparatory for the higher light and glory and blessedness which they were to receive and enjoy after Christ was glorified and the Holy Ghost was given unto them. Of the present privileges of all believers in common, our Saviour thus speaks: "He that believeth on Me, as the Scripture hath said, out of his belly shall flow rivers of living water." "But this," the apostle adds, "He spake of the Spirit, which they that believe on Him should receive; for the Holy Ghost was not yet given, because that Jesus was not yet glorified."

None, we are taught here, could have had this blessedness consummated in their experience before "Jesus was glorified." No prophet, or king, or disciple ever did enjoy, or could have enjoyed, prior to the time when the Holy Ghost was given, the light, privileges, and blessedness which all believers may now enjoy under the dispensation of the Spirit.

Such are the express teachings of our Saviour upon this subject. According to the equally express teachings of prophecy also, "He that is feeble among you at that day shall be as David, while the house of David shall be as God, as the angel of the Lord before Him." Those things, also, after which "the prophets inquired and searched diligently," were not the sayings or works of our Saviour prior to His crucifixion, but "the sufferings of Christ and the glory that should follow"—follow after "the Holy Ghost was given." The most important utterances of our Saviour were like enigmas, even to the disciples, until after "the Spirit took of the things of Christ and showed them unto them."

4. The special *mission of the Spirit*, as revealed by our Saviour Himself, next claims our attention. His mission is set forth in such words as the following: "He shall teach you all things, and bring all things to your remembrance whatsoever I have said unto you;" "He shall glorify Me; for He shall receive of Mine and shall show it unto you;" "He will guide you into all truth;" "He shall testify of Me;" "I by the Spirit will show you plainly of the Father;" "He will reprove the world of sin, of righteousness, and of judgment;" "He shall not speak of Himself, but whatsoever He shall hear, that shall He speak; and He will show you things to come;" "And they shall all be taught of God."

The mission of the Spirit, then, is to put the mind in full possession of that "eternal life," which consists in "*knowing* the only living and true God, and Jesus Christ whom He hath sent." It is one thing to study the Word of God with human helps; it is quite another thing to have in addition to these the Spirit of God, first to strengthen His truth in "the inner man," and then to open it to our vision, especially "the image of the glory of God in the face of Jesus Christ." The Church, under the power of the Spirit's indwelling and teaching, is "the light of the world." While the Church is laboring for the salvation of the race, the Spirit is in the world to convince men of sin and lead them to Christ. After they have repented and believed in Him, He sends the Comforter to enlighten, teach, help, guide, and dwell with them forever.

Prior to conversion the Spirit comes to men without being sought, and convinces them of sin, even against their will. After repentance and faith in Christ, believers receive "power from on high," "the power of the Spirit," by asking, seeking, knocking, and waiting for His coming upon them as the disciples did at the Pentecost, and as Christ did in the wilderness and in mountain solitudes.

The Spirit in Christ, in the prophets and in the apostles, gives us the whole circle and volume of revealed truth. The Spirit in the world acts as a convicting and persuading power to lead men to Christ. The Spirit in the Church abides in the hearts of all believers who seek and obtain Him, as a transforming, all-illuminating, and personal presence, through which we apprehend the things of Christ, and all truth requisite "to life and godliness," through which, as stated by the apostle, "we behold with open face the glory of God," are "changed into the same image from glory to glory," and "are filled with all the fulness of God." Such is the mission of the Spirit, as set forth by our Saviour Himself.

5. What has *Christ authorized us to expect,* through the abiding presence and power of the Spirit? This is the question which should next engage our attention. We have already spoken of the forms of Divine illumination promised by our Saviour, and which are to be received through the Spirit.

Let us now contemplate other forms of blessedness, which are pledged to us, and which are to descend to us under His ministration: "And in that day ye shall ask Me nothing. Verily, verily, I say unto you, Whatsoever ye shall ask the Father in My name, He will give it you. Hitherto ye have asked nothing in My name: ask and receive, that your joy may be full." "At that day ye shall know that I am in My Father, and ye in Me, and I in you. He that hath My commandments, and keepeth them, he it is that loveth Me; and he that loveth Me shall be loved of My Father, and I will love him, and will manifest Myself to him. Judas, not Iscariot, saith to Him, Lord, how is it that Thou wilt manifest Thyself to us, and not to the world? Jesus answered and said to him, If a man love Me, he will keep My words: and My Father will love him, and We will come to him, and make Our abode with him."

All this is spoken with direct reference to the results which were to attend the mission of the Spirit. After speaking of the illumination which believers are to receive under the teachings of the Spirit, our Saviour thus speaks of their blessedness through the Spirit's indwelling presence: "Peace I leave with you, My peace [the peace which I Myself enjoy] I give unto you." In His intercessory prayer, He thus speaks upon the same subject. "And now come I to Thee; and these things I speak in the world, that they might have My joy fulfilled in themselves." Again He adds, "And the glory which Thou hast given Me, I have given them; that they may be one, even as We are one. I in them and Thou in Me, that they may be made perfect in one; and that the world may know that Thou hast sent Me, and hast loved them, as Thou hast loved Me."

The power of the gospel in the hands of Christians, when they go forth "under the power of the Spirit," our Saviour thus describes: "Verily, verily, I say unto you, he that believeth on Me, the works that I do shall He do also; and greater works than these shall he do: because I go unto My Father." The Saviour is not here speaking of His miraculous deeds, but of the power of the gospel under His immediate ministration, as compared with the glory which was to follow His sufferings, and follow through the agency of believers when under "the power of the Spirit."

Of two individuals aiming at the same general results, one may move in a far wider sphere, and may touch a far greater number of minds, and in this sense exert a far greater influence than the other; while the influence of the latter within his narrow sphere may be in itself more efficient than that of the former. This is the great truth set before us in this memorable utterance of Christ. Each believer, the least as well as the greatest, has received from Christ a life mission and work, and has, under the power of the Spirit, an influence in itself more efficient than Christ wielded during His public ministry.

The following, then, are some of the high and glorious privileges which Christ has absolutely promised to us, provided we receive the Holy Ghost after we believe:—

1. Not only a perfect union with Him, and with the Father in Him, "the Father in Him, and He in us, and we in Him," but we are to *know* that this union between us and the adorable Trinity does exist.

2. Not only is the Spirit to "abide with us forever," but Christ and the Father will "come to us and make their abode with us;" "our fellowship," in the language of the Apostle John, "being with the Father, and with His Son Jesus Christ."

3. We are to enjoy a similar access to the throne of grace, and have the same power in prayer in our life mission and work, that Christ possessed while prosecuting His mission and work—we "asking in His name," and asking and receiving until "our joy," as His was, "is full."

4. Under the power of the Spirit we are to "bring forth much fruit" to the glory of God, and to the honor of Him that "loved us, and gave Himself for us," and thus to share in full measure the glory which the Father has given to Christ.

5. In the prosecution of our life mission and work, we, abiding and

walking in the Spirit, are to be possessed of a full fruition of that peace in God, and fulness of joy, which Christ Himself possessed, while "finishing the work which the Father had given Him to do." We should not dare to write such thoughts, did not the express words of Christ to that effect lie out in distinct utterances before our minds.

We notice, in the next place, *the plan of our Saviour,* as far as the agency of the Church is concerned in the work, of saving lost men, and bringing the world back to God. This plan may be thus stated:—

1. To organize the entire membership into one Divinely-anointed sacramental host, all of whom, in their individual and social relations, are to labor with supreme devotion for this great end.

2. To impart to each and everyone, through the Spirit, such a full and special baptism of power, as will perfectly qualify for, and adapt him to, the peculiar and special mission and work appointed him. Each individual is to be so "endued with power from on high," and so "filled with all the fulness of God," that there shall not be "a sickly or feeble one in all that host;" "the feeble among them being as David, and the house of David" (the leaders under the Great Captain of our salvation), "as the Lord, as the angel of the Lord before Him."

3. Through the abiding presence of the Spirit, and through Him of Christ and the Father in each heart, there shall exist such a visible unity of spirit, purpose, and mutual love among all the sanctified family, that the world shall believe in the divinity of our Saviour's mission.

4. To secure in all such peace, assurance, and fulness of joy, that "the Gentiles shall come to the light of the Church, and kings to the brightness of her rising."

Such is the plan, as no one will deny. What did Christ do and teach to render this plan real in the experience of the Church? In His relations as our atoning God and Saviour, He has made full provision for the complete sanctification, adequacy for every good word and work, and fulness of joy in every believer. He has purchased for each and all "the promise of the Spirit," through Whom God can do for everyone "exceeding abundantly above all that we can ask or think."

He has, by His own example, shown us how we may obtain the "sealing and earnest of the Spirit;" and how we must live and act when we go forth to our life-work under His power. He has said everything that could have been said to induce in us, first of all, supreme consecration to our life-work, and then a waiting upon God, as Christ waited before the Father, for that "enduement of power from on high" which is the immutable condition of accomplishing our Divinely-appointed mission. Among His earliest instructions we are absolutely assured of God's willingness and desire to bestow upon us this anointing when we seek and pray for it as required. We are also assured that when this baptism shall come upon us, "the days of our mourning shall be ended," and we may rejoice evermore.

Then as the time of His departure approached, His last discourse and prayer with His disciples seem to have but one leading end and aim, viz., to prepare their hearts for the reception of the Comforter, and to fix their desires and expectations upon "the glory which was to follow His sufferings."

On His first meeting with them after His resurrection, His first act, after His peace salutation, was to breathe upon them, saying, "Receive ye the Holy Ghost." After being seen of them forty days and speaking to them of the things pertaining to the "kingdom of God," after admonishing them not to "depart from Jerusalem, but wait for the promise of the Father," and assuring them that they should "be baptized with the Holy Ghost not many days hence," He finally led them out of the city as far as Bethany. There having delivered to them His final commission, "Go ye into all the world and preach the gospel to every creature," and His last command, "But tarry ye in Jerusalem until ye be endued with power from on high," He "lifted up His hands and blessed them," and then ascended upward and took His place at "the right hand of God," "leading captivity captive, and giving gifts unto men."

Now, reader, from beneath those sacred hands uplifted to bless us as well as them, those never-to-be-forgotten words, "Go," but "Tarry," come directly and personally to you and to me. Eternity is lost to us if we go not as bidden, and barrenness and spiritual blight will rest upon us if we tarry not as required. But the light of God shall attend us, and glory infinite shall encircle us at last if we do go forth as bidden on the one hand, and tarry as required on the other.

Chapter 3

Doctrine of the Baptism of the Holy Ghost Explained and Elucidated

I indeed baptize you with water unto repentance: but He that cometh after me is mightier than I, whose shoes I am not worthy to bear: He shall baptize you with the Holy Ghost, and with fire: Whose fan is in His hand, and He will throughly purge His floor, and gather His wheat into the garner; but He will burn up the chaff with unquenchable fire. —Matt. 3:11, 12

He said unto them, Have ye received the Holy Ghost since ye believed? —Acts 19:2

The preceding chapters have, we trust, opened the way for an exposition and elucidation of the doctrine of the Baptism of the Holy Ghost, as set forth in the New Testament.

In attending to this we will first of all quote the various passages of Scripture in which this doctrine is clearly set forth, and then suggest the various lessons which they appear to teach.

The *first* passage to which we refer is Acts 19:1–6: "And it came to pass that, while Apollos was at Corinth, Paul having passed through the upper coasts, came to Ephesus; and finding certain disciples, he said unto them, Have ye received the Holy Ghost since ye believed? And they said unto him, We have not so much as heard whether there be any Holy Ghost. And he said unto them, Unto what, then, were ye baptized? And they said, Unto John's baptism. Then said Paul, John verily baptized with the baptism of repentance, saying unto the people that they should believe on Him which should come after him, that is, on Christ Jesus. When they heard this they were baptized in the name of the Lord Jesus. And when Paul had laid his hands upon them, the Holy Ghost came on them; and they spake with tongues and prophesied." This passage teaches several truths of great importance in respect to the subject under consideration.

1. We learn that the gift of the Spirit was not received *in* but *after* conversion—"Have ye received the Holy Ghost *since* ye believed?"

2. We are taught that in the judgment of inspired men, believers are not fully qualified for their sphere of Christian activity until this baptism is received.

The men whom Paul met he distinctly recognized as Christians, but in want of the chief qualifications for Christian usefulness until they had been "endued with power from on high," through this Divine Baptism.

Nor was this view peculiar to Paul. It was the view of the other apostles, as we may learn from Acts 8:14–17: "Now when the apostles which were at Jerusalem heard that Samaria had received the Word of God, they sent unto them Peter and John, who, when they were come down, prayed for them, that they might receive the Holy Ghost, for as yet He was fallen upon none of them, only they were baptized in the name of the Lord Jesus. Then laid they their hands on them, and they received the Holy Ghost."

3. We learn from the passage before us, as well as from others, that when believers *do* receive this Divine Baptism, they enter at once upon forms of Christian activity and usefulness otherwise impossible to them. It was so with the twelve individuals referred to, and with the apostles and their associates at the Pentecost, and also with Apollos after he was instructed by Priscilla and Aquila.

4. We learn also that where the Holy Ghost is received such a change is wrought in the subject, that he himself is distinctly conscious of it. This change is also, with equal distinctness, seen by others. The transformation which took place in the believers in Samaria was observed even by Simon the sorcerer.

The change produced in the apostles and their associates at the Pentecost, was not only manifest to the inhabitants of Jerusalem, but to the multitudes assembled from surrounding nations. The new forms of life and activity which followed the descent of the Spirit upon the believers assembled at the house of Cornelius were at once obvious to Peter and his companions from Joppa. Acts 10:44–47: "While Peter yet spake these words, the Holy Ghost fell on all them which heard the word. And they of the circumcision which believed were astonished, as many as came with Peter, because that on the Gentiles also was poured out the gift of the Holy Ghost, for they heard them speak with tongues and magnify God. Then answered Peter, Can any man forbid water, that these should not be baptized, which have received the Holy Ghost as well as we?" That the change wrought by the gift of the Spirit should be visible to others, as well as to believers, was foreshadowed in prophecy: "The Lord shall rise upon thee, and His glory shall be seen upon thee."

5. The gift of the Spirit does not ordinarily come to believers unsought or unexpected, but where and when they are seeking it and waiting for it. We have but one case recorded in the New Testament in which this blessing came when not definitely sought. This is the case presented above—the case in which the Gentiles first received this "unspeakable gift." Here it was thus given for reasons that at once disappeared. To us, the great truth stands plainly revealed, that "the sealing and earnest of the Spirit" will not be given to us, but upon the condition that we seek it and wait for it, as the apostles and primitive Christians sought and waited for it.

The *second* passage to which we call attention is Eph. 1:13: "In whom ye also trusted, after that ye heard the word of truth, the gospel of your salvation; in whom, also, after that ye believed, ye were sealed with that Holy Spirit of promise." Here we have the order of facts as occurring in actual experience, viz., hearing, then believing, then, after believing, "the sealing with that Holy Spirit of promise." All is plain here but the meaning of the term "sealed." Reference is had, in the use of this term, to the final act of parties rendering permanently valid and mutually obligatory written covenants, in putting their hand and seal to the document.

When a penitent believes in Christ, "he sets to his seal that God is true;" then God gives His Holy Spirit unto him to seal on his heart, the fact that he is "accepted in the Beloved," and is brought into covenant relations with "the Father of lights." Until this is done he has no witness from God that his sins are blotted out and that his name is written in Heaven. It would evince great presumption in us to call ourselves His renewed and adopted children, without the testimony and sealing of His Holy Spirit. "Because ye are sons, God hath sent forth the Spirit of His Son into your hearts, crying, Abba, Father."

A *third* passage which we find on this subject is in 2 Cor. 1:22, where we read that God both "seals us and gives the *earnest* of the Spirit in our hearts." In Eph. 1:14 we read that in the gift of the Spirit we receive not only a seal of our title to sonship with God, but "the earnest of our inheritance until the redemption of the purchased possession."

The term "earnest" implies, in our language as well as in the original, two ideas—a part of the inheritance given in hand, and that as a pledge of an ultimate possession of the whole. The part received being the same in kind as the remainder, puts the recipient in possession of the same blessedness in kind which he is afterwards to receive in its fulness. This, then, is true of all who receive the "sealing and earnest of the Spirit in their hearts." With them glory is begun below. Heaven itself has dawned upon their inner life.

The *fourth* passage to which we invite attention is Eph. 3:14–21. The passage is rather long, but will repay a careful consideration, as it throws great light on our present inquires, "For this cause I bow my knees unto the Father of our Lord Jesus Christ, of whom the whole family in Heaven and earth is named, that He would grant you, according to the riches of His glory, to be strengthened with might by His Spirit in the inner man; that Christ may dwell in your hearts by faith; that ye, being rooted and grounded in love, may be able to comprehend with all saints what is the breadth, and length, and depth, and height; and to know the love of Christ, which passeth knowledge, that ye might be filled with all the fulness of God. Now unto Him that is able to do exceeding abundantly above all that we ask or think, according to the power that worketh in us, unto Him be glory in the Church by Christ Jesus throughout all ages, world without end. Amen."

The reader will notice the various stages of Christian experience here presented, and how each is preparatory to that which follows next in order, until the whole culminates in the soul being "filled with all the fulness of God." It will also be observed that this fulness results primarily from one originating cause—the indwelling of the Spirit in our hearts. Let us now contemplate these great central facts of the spiritual life, in the order here presented.

1. When we "receive the Holy Ghost, after we have believed," the first result is an expansion and accumulation of intellectual, moral, and spiritual power. Our faculties of apprehension and comprehension are greatly enlarged. In other words, we are "strengthened with might by the Spirit in the inner man." We become "strong in the Lord, and in the power of His might." We are able to think, to pray, to suffer, to submit, to do and to endure as would otherwise be impossible to us.

2. When our bodies thus become "the temples of the Holy Ghost," and we are "builded together for an habitation of God through the Spirit," Christ then "dwells in our hearts by faith," and is "in us the hope of glory." He and the Father "come to us and make their abode with us," and then "truly our fellowship is with the Father and with His Son Jesus Christ." We thus enjoy "the fellowship of the Spirit," and in this Divine fellowship we come to "know and believe the love that God hath to us" and by this means our "love is made perfect," our characters take form after the Divine image, and we become "confirmed, settled, and strengthened;" that is, we become "rooted and grounded in love."

3. When thus "walking in the light as God is in the light," "beholding with open face the glory of the Lord," and having "fellowship with the Father and with His Son Jesus Christ," we at length attain to "a comprehension of the breadth, and length, and depth, and height, and to know the love of Christ, which passeth knowledge." We, then, know by experience what our Saviour meant when He said, "And this is life eternal, that they might *know* Thee, the only true God, and Jesus Christ whom Thou hast sent."

4. As a further result, all our powers and susceptibilities, and activities become pervaded and filled with "the light of God." Our dwelling place is now in the center of an infinite fulness, where every want is met, where the "effect of righteousness is peace, and the fruit of righteousness

is quietness and assurance forever," and where "God is our everlasting light, and the days of our mourning are ended." In other words, we are "filled with all the fulness of God."

5. The inspired caution which follows must not be overlooked in this connection. When our thoughts, desires, and prayers turn towards God, we must *never* "limit the Holy One." We must *never* suppose that the measure of grace, which He shall give, will be limited by what we "ask or think."

We are to bear in mind, on the other hand, that the measure of our real necessities, not as seen by ourselves, but as they lie out under the eye of God, is the limit with which He is able to fill us, and which He will confer when we "put our trust in Him." "According to the power"—that is, by means of the power of the Spirit—"that worketh in us," God is "able to do exceeding abundantly above all that we ask or think." This is "the way of holiness," along which all are advancing who "receive the Holy Ghost *after* they have believed," and who do not "grieve" or "quench the Spirit," but "walk in the Spirit."

In addition to the above, there are various passages which speak of the *power* of the Spirit demanding special notice. The Spirit, as imparted to Christ, is called "the Spirit of wisdom and understanding, the Spirit of counsel and might, the Spirit of knowledge and of the fear of the Lord." Jesus commanded His disciples to "tarry in Jerusalem until they were endued with power from on high." Again, "Ye shall receive *power* after that the Holy Ghost is come upon you."

"Through the power of the Holy Ghost" we are "filled with all joy and peace in believing," and "abound in hope." Through the power of the Spirit the truth of God has an all-transforming influence over our whole moral and spiritual being and character. "We all, with open face beholding as in a glass the glory of the Lord, are changed into the same image from glory to glory, even as by the Spirit of the Lord."

The Spirit also has absolute control of all the elements of moral and spiritual power within us. He can purify our emotions and affections, quicken into immortal life and vigor our intellectual and executive activities, transform character and consolidate virtue, and thus render us "strong in the Lord and in the power of His might" for all purposes of thought, action, and endurance. But more of this in another chapter.

Let us now turn our attention to the memorable utterance of our Saviour, found in John 7:38, 39: "He that believeth on Me, as the Scripture hath said, out of his belly shall flow rivers of living water. But this spake He of the Spirit, which they that believe on Him should receive, for the Holy Ghost was not yet given, because that Jesus was not yet glorified." The following important truths, undeniably revealed in this passage, deserve particular attention:

1. The Spirit, with all that shall follow His reception, is here promised absolutely to every believer to the end of time. "If *any* man thirst," says Christ, in the verse preceding, "let him come unto Me, and drink." "He that believeth on Me"—that is, every individual that shall believe —"as the Scripture hath said, out of his belly shall flow rivers of living water." No promise can be more universal.

2. The Spirit, as here promised, was given to no believer until after Jesus was glorified, and never at that time in conversion, but only and exclusively AFTER he had believed to the saving of his soul.

3. Let us now think of the moral and spiritual state, "the everlasting consolations," the assurances of hope, the immortal fellowships, and fulness of joy, represented by such language as this, "Rivers of living water." "Whosoever," says our Saviour again, "drinketh of the water that I shall give him, shall never thirst; but the water that I shall give him shall be in him a well of water, springing up into everlasting life." All that such language imports becomes real in the experience of every believer who "receives the Holy Ghost" *after* he has believed.

On no other condition can such a form of life and blessedness become real in the experience of any individual. "But this He spake of the Spirit." You may possess all this, reader, because you may "be filled with the Spirit," and may "walk in the Spirit." You *must* possess all this, or your Christian life, in its essential particulars, will be a melancholy failure.

The *object* for which the Spirit is given is also specified in the New Testament. 1 Cor. 12:7: "But the manifestation of the Spirit is given to every man to profit withal;" that is, to render him efficiently useful as a member of the sanctified family. "To one," we are told, 1 Cor. 12:8–11, "is given by the Spirit the word of wisdom; to another, the word of knowledge by the same Spirit; to another, faith by the same Spirit; to another, the gifts of healing by the same Spirit; to another, the working of miracles; to another, prophecy; to another, discerning of spirits; to another, divers kinds of tongues; to another, the interpretation of tongues; but all these worketh that one and the self-same Spirit, dividing to every man severally as He will."

All who receive this baptism, we are taught (verse 13), "by one Spirit are baptized into one body," and "made to drink into one Spirit." All have not imparted to them the same gifts; but each receives, in connection with what is common to all, special gifts and influences, which adapt him to his particular place as "a member of the body of Christ." The specific object of the entire chapter before us is to elucidate this one truth.

The *spirit of prophecy* which attends this baptism requires special attention. Acts 2:18: "And on My servants and on My handmaidens I will pour out, in those days, of My Spirit; and they shall prophesy." Acts 21:9: "And the same man had four daughters, virgins, which did prophesy." The particular meaning of the term "prophesy," in the New Testament, is not to foretell future events, but, as we are informed, 1 Cor. 14:3, 4, to utter Divine truth under the illumination of the Spirit, so as to edify those that hear—the Church especially: "But he that prophesieth, speaketh unto men to edification, and exhortation, and comfort. He that speaketh in an unknown tongue, edifieth himself; but he that prophesieth, edifieth the Church."

The effect upon worldly minds of the spirit of prophecy in the Church is set forth in verses 23 and 24 of the same chapter: "If therefore the whole Church be come together into one place, and all speak with tongues, and there come in those that are unlearned, or unbelievers, will they not say that ye are mad? But if all prophesy, and there come in one that believeth not, or one unlearned, he is convinced of all, he is judged of all: and thus are the secrets of his heart made manifest; and so falling down on his face he will worship God, and report that God is in you of a truth."

This prophetic power, the power of utterance for the edification of the Church and the conversion of sinners, is in all such passages and in other Scriptures represented as the common privilege of all believers. Let any worldly person enter a circle whose hearts are full of the Holy Ghost, and he will at once recognize himself as encompassed with the light of God, and will he impressed with the fact that the kingdom of God has come nigh unto him. When *any* one speaks there will be an unction about his utterance, which all will recognize as Divine.

Another portion of the New Testament, which has an important bearing upon our present inquiries, is the first baptism of the Spirit after "Jesus was glorified;" that which occurred at the Pentecost. A full account of this event is given in the first and second chapters of Acts. The following facts in this account deserve attention:—

1. The apostles and their associates, knowing well that the promise of the Holy Spirit was about to be fulfilled, made every possible arrangement to receive Him; such as completing the required number of apostles, and the preparation of their hearts for His glorious entrance.

Having done this, they met together in perfect unity of prayer and expectation to receive "the promise of the Father." "And when the day of Pentecost was fully come, they were all with one accord in one place." Here is a revelation to us of the spiritual state in which we may expect this Divine baptism—viz., *a state of total consecration to Christ, and a waiting and praying for it with all our hearts.*

2. We notice also the signs which immediately preceded the baptism itself. First of all, the place was shaken as by a mighty rushing wind; then appeared the cloven tongues; and lastly, the internal manifestation, when all in common "were filled with the Holy Ghost." We have, we believe, but three instances in which the bestowment of this blessing was preceded by external manifestations—the anointing of Christ, the case before us, and the one after the release of Peter and John, recorded in Acts 4:31: "And when they had prayed the place was shaken where they were assembled together, and they were all filled with the Holy Ghost, and they spake the Word of God with boldness." In all other instances the manifestation was wholly *internal.*

3. We notice, again, the *special* and the common effects of this baptism—the speaking with tongues and prophesying, or the utterance of Divine truth under Divine influence. The former was a miraculous

power granted to the *few*; the latter, a special gift granted to *all* in common. Few spake with tongues; all uttered "the wonderful works of God," and "spoke the Word of God with boldness."

4. We notice, finally, in this connection, the *universality* of "the promise of the Spirit." This is manifest in the condition on which this gift of God was promised to those addressed by Peter on this occasion. Acts 2:38: "Then Peter said unto them, Repent, and be baptized, every one of you, in the name of Jesus Christ, for the remission of sins, and ye shall receive the gift of the Holy Ghost." Here we are taught that all who repent and believe in Christ, and openly confess Him, become, for this reason, graciously entitled to this promise. So the apostle positively affirms in the next verse, "For the promise is unto you and to your children, and to all that are afar off, even to as many as the Lord our God shall call." Here we have universality in its strictest and most absolute form.

One and only one other aspect of this great theme demands our notice in this connection; we refer to the doctrine of the Spirit as an *abiding presence* in the Church, and in all the membership of the same. On this subject the teachings of our Saviour are very specific. John 14:16: "And I will pray the Father, and He will give you another Comforter, that He may abide with you forever."

The visible presence of Christ with His disciples was temporary: that of the Spirit was to be perpetual; and the blessings received through the presence of the Spirit were to be much greater than those received through the personal presence of Christ. John 16:7: "Nevertheless I tell you the truth; it is expedient for you that I go away: for if I go not away, the Comforter will not come unto you; but if I depart, I will send Him unto you."

Such is the doctrine of the Spirit, as presented in the Scriptures of truth. Let us now attend to certain general suggestions tending to elucidate still further this great subject.

We will consider:—

I. THE NATURE OF THE PROMISE OF THE SPIRIT

1. The Spirit, as the crowning glory and promise of the New Dispensation, is not, although supernatural, any form of *miraculous*

power. As a miracle-working power, He had been in the Church ever since the fall, and had been imparted as such to the disciples prior to the death of Christ; yet as promised by our Saviour, and foretold by the prophets, He was not given until after "Christ was glorified." The baptism at the Pentecost was the beginning of the fulfillment of this promise.

2. The Spirit sustains one relation to the world and quite another to the Church. To the former He was a convicting and converting power; to the latter He is an all-illuminating, all-sanctifying, and all-strengthening presence, through whom we are continuously transformed into the Divine image "from glory to glory," brought into "fellowship with the Father and with His Son Jesus Christ," have a continuous earnest of eternal fruition, and are "filled with all the fulness of God."

3. The promise of the Spirit does not pertain merely to the apostles, the Primitive Church, or a favored few in subsequent ages. It is, on the other hand, the *common* gift to all who believe in Christ, the least as well as the greatest, and that to the end of time. Nothing can be more specific than the teachings of the Scriptures on this subject. "All thy children shall be taught of the Lord, and great shall be the peace of thy children;" "The promise is to you and to your children, and to *all* that are afar off, even to as many as the Lord our God shall call;" "He that believeth on Me (as the Scriptures have said), out of his belly shall flow rivers of living water. But this He spake of the Spirit, which they that believe on Him should receive."

4. While all who believe become thereby entitled to this promise, its fulfillment is to be sought by faith *after* we have believed in Jesus; just as pardon is sought in conversion. The promise is as absolute in one case as in the other. There is nothing which God so desires to bestow upon sinners as pardon, and with it eternal life. Neither is there any gift He is more willing to bestow upon believers than this Divine Baptism. Here all who ask receive, and all who seek find. Nothing but unbelief can prevent pardon; and nothing but a want of faith in the promise of God can prevent an "enduement of power from on high."

5. There is no natural, or intellectual, or educational, or moral, or ecclesiastical gift which can be a substitute for this. It is the all-essential and absolutely supreme gift of God in this dispensation. As the sun in the

solar system, and life in the human body are the highest good, and nothing can supersede them; so this baptism is the noblest blessing of Christianity, and no other can fill its place.

II. SOME OF THE EFFECTS OF THIS BAPTISM

In reference to the effects of this baptism, we would remark in general, that *permanence and power* are the leading characteristics. Without this, feebleness characterizes the strongest among us; with it, "he that is feeble among us is as David, and the house of David, as the Lord, as the angel of the Lord before him." In the former state, "our souls can neither fly nor go;" in the latter, "we mount up on wings as eagles, we run and are not weary, and walk and are not faint." In the former state "we walk in darkness," in the latter "God is our everlasting light, and the days of our mourning are ended." In the former state we are weary, "tossed with tempests, and not comforted;" in the latter, "our peace is as a river, and our righteousness as the waves of the sea." In the former state doubts and fears prevail, in the latter we walk in the cloudless sunlight of "the full assurance of hope." In the one state we groan and sigh, and "weep for sorrow of heart," in the other "we sing for joy of heart," returning and coming "to Zion with songs and everlasting joy upon our heads."

To be more particular, we remark:—

1. In this state all our *natural powers* are quickened and developed into unwonted activity and energy. When in the presence of great minds, great thoughts, deep emotions, and vast energies of action, all our mental powers take on forms of activity otherwise impossible to us. What, then, must be the effect upon our mental faculties when they are all brought consciously under the influence of the infinite and eternal mind, and move and act under the power of God's thoughts, emotions, and activities?

These statements are all sustained by universal observation and experience. Whenever anyone receives this baptism, a radical change is immediately observed in the forms which his actions assume. Thought is expanded, emotion deepened, and activity energized as never before.

2. Especially is there an increase of *moral* and *spiritual* power to endure and accomplish all things according to the Divine will. Without

this baptism the mind remains in servitude to the natural propensities, faints under chastisements, is overcome when tempted, and rendered despondent through broken resolutions. Under this baptism we have a sovereign control over our spirit, we endure when tried, overcome when tempted, and when weak in ourselves find everlasting strength in God.

Power with God and with men is an invariable result of this anointing. After Luther received it, his enemies were accustomed to say that he could obtain anything from God for which he asked. After Knox received it, Mary Queen of Scots was accustomed to say that she feared the prayers of that one man more than she did the fleets and armies of Elizabeth. So it was with the apostles and first Christians after the Pentecost. Who among men could "resist the wisdom and the spirit with which they spake?" The same is true of the weakest in the churches when thus baptized with the Holy Ghost.

3. *Soul-transforming apprehensions of truth* is another marked result of this baptism. Void of this anointing, the Bible, in its spiritual teachings, seems to be a sealed book, or a dead letter. With it, every truth has an all-vitalizing power to quicken and enlarge thought, to deepen spiritual emotion, to quicken the mental faculties, and to transform the whole moral and spiritual being and character. We walk in the light of God, which, shining upon the sacred page, gives to its truth a cleansing, illuminating, elevating, and energizing effect upon our souls. We realize the force of what Paul teaches as the result of receiving the Spirit in 1 Cor. 2:9–16.

4. *Absolute assurance of hope* is another equally marked result of this baptism. This assurance is represented by such forms of expression as these: "We *know* that we are of God," "we *know* that we have passed from death unto life," "we *know* in whom we have believed," and "truly our fellowship is with the Father, and with His Son Jesus Christ." "Now we have received, not the spirit which is of the world, but the Spirit which is of God, that we might *know* the things which are freely given to us of God." After the believer has received the witness of the Spirit, he can no more doubt his adoption than he can doubt his own being. There is nothing of which he does or can enjoy a more absolute assurance.

5. Another result of this baptism is conscious "*fellowship with the*

Father, and with His Son Jesus Christ." Before the believer has received the Holy Ghost, Christ is to his apprehension far off in Heaven, and God is at an infinite remove. After this baptism, the soul becomes a temple of the Triune Deity. God then "walks in us and dwells in us." The Father and the Son "come to us and make their abode with us," and we are thus "filled with all the fulness of God." Christ is in us the hope of glory, and dwells in our hearts by faith. In prayer, we speak to Him as a personal presence, and inwardly "see His face." God "shines in our hearts, to give the light of the knowledge of the glory of God in the face of Jesus Christ." We know then, and only then, what Christ means when He says, "I will come to you," "I will manifest Myself to him," and "I will come unto him and sup with him, and he with Me," and "I will not leave you comfortless: I will come to you."

6. We mention as another result, *deep and permanent spiritual blessedness.* This blessedness is set forth by such Divine expressions as "joy in God," "joy in tribulation," "rejoice evermore," "pleasure in infirmities, in reproaches, in necessities, in persecutions, in distresses for Christ's sake," "everlasting consolations and good hope through grace," "joy unspeakable, and full of glory," "the peace of God, which passeth understanding, keeps our minds and hearts through Christ Jesus," "peace as a river, and righteousness as the waves of the sea," and "the Lord shall be their everlasting light, and the days of their mourning shall be ended." In short, when we have received the Holy Ghost after we have believed, our interior life will fully correspond with Christian experience, as foreseen by the ancient prophets and as described in the New Testament.

7. Christian unity and love is another result which will follow this baptism. We shall "have fellowship" not only "with the Father, and with His Son Jesus Christ," but also "one with another;" and the prayer of the Saviour in behalf of His people will be fully answered: "That they all may be one; as Thou, Father, art in Me, and I in Thee, that they also may be one in us; that the world may believe that Thou hast sent Me;" "I in them, and Thou in Me, that they may be made perfect in one; and that the world may know that Thou hast sent Me, and hast loved them, as Thou hast loved Me."

It is vain to look for such a condition of unity and concord as here prayed for only as the glorious fruits of a baptism of the Holy Ghost. Any other spirit than this will produce division and strife; but this running through every member will bring the whole as a body to the Head, fitly joined together and compacted, so that there shall be no schism in the body.

III. CONDITIONS ON WHICH THIS BAPTISM MAY BE OBTAINED

In the expositions above given, the conditions on which this Divine baptism may be obtained have been rendered so plain, that only a few particulars need be specified under this division of our subject. It may be stated as a general principle of the Divine administration, and especially in connection with the gift of the Spirit, that no such blessing is conferred until its value is appreciated, until there is faith in the provisions and promises of grace in respect to it, and until it is specifically sought as a supreme good. What, then, are the conditions on which we may receive this all-crowning gift of Divine grace? They are, among others, the following:—

1. It must be clearly separated in thought from all miraculous endowments, and from that form of Divine influence which issues in conversion and justification. What if the disciples, when told to "tarry in Jerusalem until they were endued with power from on high," had replied, "Lord we have the Spirit already, we have His miraculous gifts, and His converting influence has never left us." Would they have obtained the Pentecostal baptism? Assuredly not. Having such a state of mind, would any of the individuals subsequently addressed by the apostles upon this subject have been filled with the Spirit?

So with us at the present time. God has so clearly distinguished and separated this from all other gifts of grace and forms of Divine manifestation that, until we have distinctly recognized and credited what He has revealed upon the subject, we are not prepared to receive the blessing, and have no reason to expect it.

2. We must distinctly recognize ourselves, on account of our having exercised "repentance towards God, and faith in our Lord Jesus Christ," as formally entitled to plead "the promise of the Spirit," with the

absolute certainty of receiving it. This is the distinctly revealed birthright of every believer.

3. In a state of supreme consecration to Christ, we must plead this promise before God, and watch for it and wait for it, as the disciples did at Jerusalem, until the baptism comes upon us. Here, all reap who faint not. Reader, "the highway of holiness" is now open before you. Will you walk in it? Will you tarry before God until you, for your life-mission and work, are "endued with power from on high?"

4. If as churches or as a body of believers we seek this baptism of the Holy Ghost, we must *each* meet the conditions above-named, so that we may appear before God for this blessing as the apostles and their associates—viz., "all continue with one accord in prayer and supplication." "And when the day of Pentecost was fully come, they were all with one accord in one place." Thus must we wait, pray, supplicate, and believe until the promise of the Father fall upon us as upon them at the beginning. And thus waiting, it will not be "many days" ere the Heavenly Gift come down, and we shall all be "filled with the Holy Ghost."

CHAPTER 4

Baptisms of the Spirit Under the Old and New Dispensations Compared

And it shall come to pass afterward, that I will pour out My Spirit upon all flesh; and your sons and your daughters shall prophesy, your old men shall dream dreams, your young men shall see visions: And also upon the servants and upon the handmaids in those days will I pour out My Spirit. —Joel 2:28, 29

But this spake He of the Spirit, which they that believe on Him should receive: for the Holy Ghost was not yet given; because that Jesus was not yet glorified. —John 7:39

At "sundry times" of the Old Testament Dispensation, we have accounts of baptisms of the Spirit analogous to those which occurred after "Christ was glorified." Yet we are told that until after this event "the Holy Ghost was not yet given." There must be something very peculiar about this last baptism. To show the nature of this peculiarity is the object of this chapter. In doing so, we will first of all give the historic facts as they occur in the Scriptures.

Of Enoch we read that for three hundred years he "walked with God." To have done this he must have enjoyed certain forms and degrees of "the communion and fellowship of the Spirit." When Abraham (Gen. 15:7) was made distinctly conscious that God was "his shield and exceeding great reward," he must have entered into a new form of spiritual life in God. This was to him a special baptism of the Spirit; and he had others equally memorable during the progress of his natural life.

Jacob also received a baptism of the Spirit, such as was given under the Old Testament Dispensation. During his sojourn at Bethel, he obtained a baptism which gave an entirely new direction to his inward experience and outward conduct. It was through this baptism that afterwards, "as a Prince, he had power with God and with man, and prevailed."

One of the most memorable instances of an Old Testament baptism of the Spirit is recorded of Moses in Exodus 33 and 34. After informing us that "The Lord spake unto Moses face to face, as a man speaketh unto his friend," we have the following remarkable statements:—"And Moses said unto the Lord, See, Thou sayest unto me, Bring up this people: and Thou hast not let me know whom Thou wilt send with me. Yet Thou hast said, I know thee by name, and thou hast also found grace in My sight. Now therefore, I pray Thee, if I have found grace in Thy sight, show me now Thy way, that I may know Thee, that I may find grace in Thy sight: and consider that this nation is Thy people. And He said, My presence shall go with thee, and I will give thee rest. And he said unto Him, If Thy presence go not with me, carry us not up hence. For wherein shall it be known here that I and Thy people have found grace in Thy sight? Is it not in that Thou goest with us? So shall we be separated, I and Thy people, from all the people that are upon the face of the earth. And the Lord said unto Moses, I will do this thing also that thou hast spoken; for thou hast found grace in My sight, and I know thee by name. And he said, I beseech Thee, show me Thy glory. And He said, I will make all My goodness pass before thee, and I will proclaim the name of the Lord before thee; and will be gracious to whom I will be gracious, and will show mercy on whom I will show mercy. And He said, Thou canst not see My face: for there shall no man see Me, and live. And the Lord said, Behold, there is a place by Me, and thou shalt stand upon a rock: and it shall come to pass, while My glory passeth by, that I will put thee in a cleft of the rock, and will cover thee with My hand while I pass by; and I will take away Mine hand, and thou shalt see My back parts; but My face shall not be seen."

Here, then, we have the waiting and supplication of Moses, with the express promise of Jehovah to him. Let us now see the baptism itself, in which the Divine promise was fulfilled (Exodus 34):—"And the Lord descended in the cloud, and stood with him there, and proclaimed the name of the Lord. And the Lord passed by before him, and proclaimed, The Lord, the Lord God, merciful and gracious, longsuffering, and abundant in goodness and truth, keeping mercy for thousands, forgiving iniquity and transgression and sin, and that will by no means clear the guilty; visiting the iniquity of the fathers upon the children, and upon the children's children, unto the third and to the fourth generation. And Moses made haste, and bowed his head towards the earth, and worshipped."

From that moment onward Moses was a *new* man. He felt, spoke, and acted as it was impossible for him to have done before. Prior to this he had known God as the Creator and universal Lawgiver, and had received from Him the power of working miracles, together with the Spirit of revelation. Yet he had never, in the true and proper sense, "*known* God" or "understood His way;" and more especially was he ignorant of what constituted the *essential glory* of the Divine character. Thenceforth the glory of God was the everlasting light of his soul.

We would now direct attention to Num. 11:24–30, where we have an account of the baptism given to the seventy elders, who were selected to aid Moses in ruling and teaching the people. The prophetic spirit here vouchsafed was not that of foretelling future events, but of speaking Divine truth under special Divine influences. Let us read the passage attentively:—"And Moses went out, and told the people the words of the Lord, and gathered the seventy men of the elders of the people, and set them round about the tabernacle. And the Lord came down in a cloud, and spake unto him, and took of the spirit that was upon him, and gave it unto the seventy elders: and it came to pass, that, when the spirit rested upon them, they prophesied, and did not cease. But there remained two of the men in the camp, the name of the one was Eldad, and the name of the other Medad: and the Spirit rested upon them; and they were of them that were written, but went not out unto the tabernacle; and they prophesied in the camp. And there ran a young man, and told Moses, and said, Eldad and Medad do prophesy in the camp. And Joshua the son of Nun, the servant of Moses, one of his young men, answered and said,

My lord Moses, forbid them. And Moses said unto him, Enviest thou for my sake? Would God that all the Lord's people were prophets, and that the Lord would put His Spirit upon them! And Moses gat him into the camp, he and the elders of Israel."

We learn from this passage that none do or can prophesy, as God's servants, who have not this baptism, and that all who do receive it are so filled with Divine truth and power that they must speak forth "the wondrous works of God," and "magnify the Lord." Truth apprehended through the illumination of the Spirit is "as a fire shut up in the bones." All such must speak of their views and feelings of God, of the love of Christ, and of the glories of redemption.

The next case to which we would call attention is the baptism given to Saul, after Samuel had anointed him king (1 Sam. 10:9–13):—"And it was so, that when he had turned his back to go from Samuel, God gave him another heart: and all those signs came to pass that day. And when they came hither to the hill, behold, a company of prophets met him; and the Spirit of God came upon him, and he prophesied among them. And it came to pass, when all that knew him beforetime saw that, behold, he prophesied among the prophets, then the people said one to another, What is this that is come unto the son of Kish? Is Saul also among the prophets? And one of the same place answered and said, But who is their father? Therefore it became a proverb, Is Saul also among the prophets? And when he had made an end of prophesying, he came to the high place."

The new heart given to Saul was not, we suppose, a holy but kingly state of mind, by which he was fully qualified for his new office. The prophetic Spirit, of which he became at the time possessed, was the common result of a temporary or permanent baptism of the Spirit. One great truth is presented in this passage in regard to the Divine anointing. It always imparts special qualifications for specific spheres of usefulness. In 1 Sam. 19:18–23, we have a striking instance in which temporary baptisms come upon wicked men:—"So David fled, and escaped, and came to Samuel to Ramah, and told him all that Saul had done to him. And he and Samuel went and dwelt in Naioth. And it was told Saul, saying, Behold, David is at Naioth in Ramah. And Saul sent messengers to take

David: and when they saw the company of the prophets prophesying, and Samuel standing as appointed over them, the Spirit of God was upon the messengers of Saul, and they also prophesied. And when it was told Saul, he sent other messengers, and they prophesied likewise. And Saul sent messengers again the third time, and they prophesied also. Then went he also to Ramah, and came to a great well that is in Sechu: and he asked and said, Where are Samuel and David? And one said, Behold, they be at Naioth in Ramah. And he went thither to Naioth in Ramah: and the Spirit of God was upon him also, and he went on, and prophesied, until he came to Naioth in Ramah."

A similar spirit, we are told, came upon Balaam, under which he uttered, for the time, just such truths as God dictated.

In 2 Kings 2:9–15 we have an account of the special baptism which Elisha received, and by which he was prepared for the prophetic office:—"And it came to pass, when they were gone over, that Elijah said unto Elisha, Ask what I shall do for thee, before I be taken away from thee. And Elisha said, I pray thee, let a *double* portion of thy spirit be upon me. And he said, Thou hast asked a hard thing: nevertheless, if thou see me when I am taken from thee, it shall be so unto thee; but if not, it shall not be so. And it came to pass, as they still went on, and talked, that, behold, there appeared a chariot of fire, and horses of fire, and parted them both asunder; and Elijah went up by a whirlwind into Heaven. And Elisha saw it, and he cried, My father, my father, the chariot of Israel, and the horsemen thereof. And he saw him no more: and he took hold of his own clothes, and rent them in two pieces. He took up also the mantle of Elijah that fell from him, and went back, and stood by the bank of Jordan; and he took the mantle of Elijah that fell from him, and smote the waters, and said, Where is the Lord God of Elijah? And when he also had smitten the waters, they parted hither and thither: and Elisha went over. And when the sons of the prophets which were to view at Jericho saw him, they said, The spirit of Elijah doth rest on Elisha. And they came to meet him, and bowed themselves to the ground before him."

From the moment the spirit of Elijah fell upon Elisha his prophetic life commenced. Under the baptism then received, and which was perpetuated, he became the most wonderful man of his age and country.

The preceding account is of considerable importance, as indicating the state of mind in which this baptism is obtained. Elisha was fully impressed with the conviction that he was to succeed Elijah as the prophet of the Lord. Hence his firm determination not to be separated from him until through him he had received the requisite "enduement of power from on high." So when we regard ourselves as "called of God to be saints," and as such also called to fill some sphere of usefulness in "God's kingdom," then under a deep impression that "we are not sufficient of ourselves to think anything as of ourselves, but that our sufficiency is of God," we resolvedly fix our hearts, as Elisha did, upon "the promise of the Spirit, the baptism of fire is near at hand."

Let us now glance at those instances of special baptisms of the Spirit which are recorded in the New Testament, and which occurred before the time when Christ was glorified. In Luke 1:67–79, after the circumcision of John, we have the following account of the baptism received by his father Zacharias:—"And his father Zacharias was filled with the Holy Ghost, and prophesied, saying, Blessed be the Lord God of Israel; for He hath visited and redeemed His people, and hath raised up an horn of salvation for us in the house of His servant David; as He spake by the mouth of His holy prophets, which have been since the world began: that we should be saved from our enemies, and from the hand of all that hate us; to perform the mercy promised to our fathers, and to remember His holy covenant; the oath which He sware to our father Abraham, that He would grant unto us, that we being delivered out of the hand of our enemies might serve Him without fear, in holiness and righteousness before Him, all the days of our life. And thou, child, shalt be called the prophet of the Highest: for thou shalt go before the face of the Lord to prepare His ways; to give knowledge of salvation unto His people by the remission of their sins, through the tender mercy of our God, whereby the day-spring from on high hath visited us, to give light to them that sit in darkness and in the shadow of death, to guide our feet into the way of peace."

The following (Luke 1:39–55) is an account of the baptism and its results which came upon Elizabeth and Mary when they met in the house of the former:—"And Mary arose in those days, and went into the hill country with haste, into a city of Juda; and entered into the house of Zacharias, and saluted Elizabeth. And it came to pass, that, when Elizabeth heard the salutation of Mary, the babe leaped in her womb; and Elizabeth was filled with the Holy Ghost: and she spake out with a loud voice, and said, Blessed art thou among women, and blessed is the fruit of thy womb. And whence is this to me, that the mother of my Lord should come to me? For, lo, as soon as the voice of thy salutation sounded in mine ears, the babe leaped in my womb for joy. And blessed is she that believed: for there shall be a performance of those things which were told her from the Lord. And Mary said, My soul doth magnify the Lord, and my spirit hath rejoiced in God my Saviour. For He hath regarded the low estate of His handmaiden: for, behold, from henceforth all generations shall call me blessed. For He that is mighty hath done to me great things; and holy is His name. And His mercy is on them that fear Him from generation to generation. He hath showed strength with His arm; He hath scattered the proud in the imagination of their hearts. He hath put down the mighty from their seats, and exalted them of low degree. He hath filled the hungry with good things; and the rich He hath sent empty away. He hath holpen His servant Israel, in remembrance of His mercy; as He spake to our fathers, to Abraham, and to his seed forever."

How similar are the results stated in the above cases to those which followed the gift of the Holy Spirit after "Christ was glorified!" "They heard them speak with tongues and magnify God." "And they spake with tongues, and prophesied." "And the disciples were filled with joy and with the Holy Ghost." "Out of his belly shall flow rivers of living waters." Also the leading idea included in the term "prophesy," as that term is used in both Testaments, is brought out in the passages above quoted. It is not revealing future events, though this often attended this baptism, but an uttering Divine truths under the immediate influence of the Holy Spirit, and, as Paul says, speaking unto men to "edification, and exhortation, and comfort." (1 Cor. 14:3) Neither does this gift necessarily include any miraculous endowment, though this has sometimes accompanied it; but it is that inward Divine illumination and manifestation in which "God becomes our everlasting light, and the days of our mourning are ended."

But while "the baptisms of the Spirit" under the two dispensations were thus similar, we shall find an essential difference between them if we consider what is said upon the subject in the New Testament. The following is Peter's statement:—"Of which salvation the prophets have inquired and searched diligently, who prophesied of the grace that should come unto you; searching what, or what manner of time the Spirit of Christ which was in them did signify, when it testified beforehand the sufferings of Christ, and the glory that should follow. Unto whom it was revealed, that not unto themselves, but unto us they did minister the things, which are now reported unto you by them that have preached the gospel unto you with the Holy Ghost sent down from Heaven, which things the angels desire to look into." (1 Pet. 1:10–12)

Paul informs us that God has reserved better things for us than the ancient saints enjoyed, and that it was only by anticipating and believing in what we have received that they were rendered perfect:—"And these all, having obtained a good report through faith, received not the promise: God having provided some better thing for us, that they without us should not be made perfect." (Heb. 11:39, 40)

John, in his gospel (7:39), teaches us that the Holy Ghost, as promised under the New, was not given under the Old Dispensation.

We may now glance definitely at the difference between these two forms of baptism, and show in what sense the Holy Ghost was not given until after Christ was glorified. As preparatory to this, let us read that special prophecy, of the fulfillment of which the baptism at the Pentecost was the commencement.

Acts 2:14–18:—"But Peter, standing up with the eleven, lifted up his voice, and said unto them, Ye men of Judaea, and all ye that dwell at Jerusalem, be this known unto you, and hearken to my words: for these are not drunken, as ye suppose, seeing it is but the third hour of the day. But this is that which was spoken by the prophet Joel: And it shall come to pass in the last days, saith God, I will pour out of My Spirit upon all flesh; and your sons and your daughters shall prophesy, and your young men shall see visions, and your old men shall dream dreams; and on My servants and on My handmaidens I will pour out in those days of My Spirit, and they shall prophesy."

These two forms of baptism differ essentially from each other in the following particulars:

1. In *extent*. Under the Old Dispensation such special anointings were granted only to a few individuals; but under the New this gift is universal as a privilege to be enjoyed by all Christ's people. What Moses *desired* might be universal then becomes universal now; "Would God that all the Lord's people were prophets, and that the Lord would pour His Spirit upon them." "The promise of the Spirit" now hangs over "all flesh." All God's people under the gospel are privileged, and required to become "the Lord's prophets;" and being all in common "filled with the Spirit," to "speak unto men to edification, and exhortation, and comfort." In this important form the Holy Ghost had never before been promised or given.

2. There is another distinction equally important. We refer to that of *permanency*. Under the Old Dispensation the prophetic baptisms were "like angels' visits, few and far between." For long periods, we are informed, the Church had no prophets and "no teaching priests." Under the New Dispensation the Spirit is to be in the Church as a *perpetually* abiding presence to the end of time; "I will pray the Father, and He shall give you another Comforter, that He may abide with you forever."

The essential design of God, in this dispensation, is that the prophetic office, as we have defined it, shall never cease, and that it shall be as extensive as the real membership of the church. What an important difference we have here between these two dispensations!

3. But the great peculiarity which distinguishes these two dispensations is the relative power of the Spirit's manifestations in each.

Under the Old Dispensation, the glory of God was only partially revealed. Hence the power which the Spirit could use for these ends was comparatively feeble. Under the present Dispensation, through the revelation of "the glory of God in the face of Jesus Christ," all of God that can be revealed to creatures in our circumstances has been made manifest: "Life and immortality have been brought to light through the gospel." "No man hath seen God at any time." "The only begotten Son who is in the bosom of the Father, He hath declared Him."

When, therefore, "the Spirit takes of the things of Christ and shows them unto us," so that we "behold, with open face, the glory of the Lord;" when He brings us into "fellowship with the Father and with His Son Jesus Christ," and God and Christ, through the Spirit, "come to us, and make their abode with us;" when He unveils to our vision "the New Jerusalem coming down from God out of Heaven;" when He enables us to comprehend the breadth, and length, and depth, and height, and to "know the love of Christ, which passeth knowledge," and "fills us with all the fulness of God"—then "the communion and fellowship," "the sealing and earnest," and all "the manifestations of the Spirit," are so new, so removed from, and so infinitely superior to anything known in the Church before, that it may truly and properly be said, that until after Christ was glorified, "the Holy Ghost had not yet been given." After this event we have a New Dispensation, and, as a consequence, a new mission of the Spirit.

We now clearly see why it is that many Christians magnify the privileges of Old Testament saints, and especially those of the apostles prior to the death of Christ, and speak of these as even more highly privileged than we now are. The former were witnesses of wondrous miracles, listened to the prophets, and sometimes even to angels; while the latter heard Christ Himself, and were eye-witnesses of His mighty works. No wonder that they were "holy men of God."

No Christian who "has received the Holy Ghost since he believed" ever entertained such a thought as that. The means of sanctification, consolation, and "fulness of joy" within the sphere of our faith and use, were wholly unknown to them; nor had the chiefest apostle, after Christ was glorified, any advantage in these respects beyond the least of all the saints now. The high and holy blessings of this Dispensation are not obtained and enjoyed through "mighty signs and wonders," talking with prophets, or through "angels' visits," but "by the power of the Holy Ghost;" and this all-sanctifying power God is ready to pour out upon us, in all the fulness that He did upon the apostles. "If thou canst believe, all things are possible to him that believeth."

We may now judge of the degree of spiritual power which was expected under the Old, and is expected under the New Dispensation.

The lowest that may now be expected is equal to the highest then; while the highest may make us like the sons of God before the throne. "He that is feeble among them at that day shall be as David, and the house of David shall be as God, as the angel of the Lord before Him."

What, then, is the main cause of the present feebleness of our churches? It is because this great truth is not sufficiently recognized and believed, and still more, because its experience is so little sought, and much less enjoyed. What meaning do most Christians now attach to the question: "Have ye received the Holy Ghost since ye believed?" Almost as little as if they "had never heard whether there be any Holy Ghost."

We notice, also, the difference between the experience of the primitive and the modern Church, and the cause of that difference. The leading theme of the former was the doctrine we are now considering. Hence the disciples were then "filled with joy and the Holy Ghost." Now this doctrine has gone into a deep and dark eclipse. As a consequence, many believers "walk in darkness and have no light," sigh after their first love, weep in sorrowful widowhood under the bondage of sin, and know almost nothing of the hidden life in the soul, but "an aching void."

When the primitive Church was scattered abroad, all its members "went everywhere preaching the Word;" now, when our members emigrate to another land, or even change the locality of their residence in their own country, many of them leave not only their religion, but their profession behind them—some of them carrying not the love of Christ, but of gold, in their hearts. This state of things will continue until this glorious doctrine of the Spirit is everywhere understood, preached, and realized in the Church.

But this condition of the Church shall not continue. In answer to the waiting, the praying; and the believing of His faithful people, God will baptize His Church with the Holy Ghost, and she will make in these last days rapid strides towards the millennium. Then shall the glory of the Lord cover the nations. "Conceive," says Mr. Barnes, "of the brightest form of experience known to the best Christian in his best hours now. Conceive of this state as increased to the full extent of the soul's capacities, and then conceive of this as the common and perpetual experience of all the Church, and then you may have some feeble conception of the coming millennium." We will only add, "Even so come, Lord Jesus, come quickly. Amen."

We add but one thought more. We. refer to "the power of the Spirit," for sanctification, consolation, and fulness of joy, now, and in *apostolic times*. That power, instead of being less, is much greater now than it was then. All that they had, we have, together with all of "our God and His Christ" that has been made manifest through the word and providence of God since that time. The power of the Spirit, as represented in prophecy, is a perpetually accumulating power. This, great central truth of the present dispensation is specifically set forth in the 47th chapter of Ezekiel by means of the emblem of "a pure river of the water of life," issuing from the threshold of the house of God; a river flowing eastward, with perpetual accumulations, filled with life and food for man, fertilizing the whole country through which it flows, and healing even the waters of the Dead Sea. We cite a few verses from this wonderful chapter:—

"Afterward he brought me again unto the door of the house; and, behold, waters issued out from under the threshold of the house eastward: for the forefront of the house stood toward the east, and the waters came down from under, from the right side of the house, at the south side of the altar. Then brought he me out of the way of the gate northward, and led me about the way without unto the outer gate by the way that looketh eastward; and, behold, there ran out waters on the right side. And when the man that had the line in his hand went forth eastward, he measured a thousand cubits, and he brought me through the waters; the waters were to the ankles. Again he measured a thousand, and brought me through the waters; the waters were to the knees. Again he measured a thousand, and brought me through; the waters were to the loins. Afterward he measured a thousand; and it was a river that I could not pass over: for the waters were risen, waters to swim in, a river that could not be passed over." "The golden age" of the Church is not in the past, but in the future. There should be no sickly nor imbecile believers now. Everyone should be strong in the Lord and in the power of His might—should be able to do all things through Christ who strengtheneth him. May this all-empowering baptism come down upon every believer in the Lord Jesus!

CHAPTER 5

Baptism of the Spirit Under the New Dispensation

But we are bound to give thanks alway to God for you, brethren beloved of the Lord, because God hath from the beginning chosen you to salvation through sanctification of the Spirit and belief of the truth. —2 Thess. 2:13

God having provided some better thing for us, that they without us should not be made perfect. —Heb. 11:40

In the last chapter some light, we hope, was thrown upon the forms and degrees in which the baptism of the Spirit was and is given under the Old and New Dispensations. But so much superior is this gift under the latter, that the apostle's statement is proper and significant—viz., "the Holy Ghost was not given until after Jesus was glorified." This superiority is a leading theme of the inspirations of the prophets and of the apostles.

This baptism, with its results in the Church and upon the world, is "the glory which was to follow the sufferings of Christ." These are "the better things that God hath reserved for us." They comprise the glory of this Christian age. "What sort of persons ought we to be," upon whom and to whom this glory has descended? That far more is expected and justly required of us than was possible to the saints under the Old Dispensation we argue from the following considerations:—

1. We live in a dispensation of far greater *light* and *knowledge* than they did. They had the Old Testament only. We have the Old and the

New combined. The former differs from the latter, as the first glimmer of dawn differs from the light of cloudless noon. They knew nothing of Christ but what was obscurely hinted through types and shadows, and prophetic revelations, which the prophets themselves did not fully comprehend. "We behold, with open face, the glory of the Lord." The way of holiness was to them very obscure and intricate. We walk in the King's highway, in which a "wayfaring man, though a fool, shall not err." With them, *midday* light was but a *feeble twilight*. With us, even "*at evening time there is light.*" *Our moon far outshines their sun.* "Life and immortality are brought to light through the gospel."

2. The *law of duty* is revealed to us in far *clearer* and more *attractive* and *impressive* forms than it was to them. To them it was revealed almost exclusively in the perceptive form, "line upon line, precept upon precept, here a little and there a little." That same law comes to us not merely in the form of command and prohibition, but also as exemplified in all its applications, through the pure and spotless example of Christ. They were taught *what* to do. We are taught not only *what* to do, but *how* to do it.

3. The *forms* of truth, hidden from them and revealed to us, have a *quickening* and *transforming* power which they did not possess as revealed and believed under the Old Dispensation. Through the greater light now shed upon them, they are far more effective in this age than they were in the times of the patriarchs and the prophets.

The Apostle John, in comparing the present with the former Dispensation, tells us that "the darkness has passed, and the true light now shineth." Peter tells us that the prophets, who stood amidst the clearest light then vouchsafed, "inquired and searched diligently, searching what, or what manner of time the Spirit of Christ which was in them did signify, when it testified beforehand of the sufferings of Christ, and the glory which should follow. Unto whom it was revealed that not unto themselves, but unto us they did minister the things which are now reported unto you by them that have preached the gospel unto you, with the Holy Ghost sent down from Heaven, which things the angels desire to look into." (1 Pet. 1:10, 11)

How impressive is the contrast which Paul draws between these dispensations: "For ye are not come unto the mount that might be touched, and that burned with fire, nor unto blackness, and darkness, and tempest, and the sound of a trumpet, and the voice of words." "But ye are come unto Mount Sion, and unto the city of the living God, the heavenly Jerusalem, and to an innumerable company of angels, to the general assembly and Church of the firstborn, which are written in Heaven, and to God, the Judge of all, and to the spirits of just men made perfect, and to Jesus the Mediator of the new covenant, and to the blood of sprinkling, that speaketh better things than that of Abel. See that ye refuse not Him that speaketh; for if they escaped not that refused Him that spake on earth, much more shall not we escape, if we turn away from Him that speaketh from Heaven." (Heb. 12:18–25)

The Scriptures everywhere represent the gospel as not only shedding new light upon questions pertaining to God, Christ, the Holy Spirit, duty, sin, holiness, redemption, and immortality, but as revealing forms of truth which have power before unknown, for conversion, sanctification, consolation, and fulness of joy.

One prophet speaks of these new revelations as "a fountain opened to the house of David, and to the inhabitants of Jerusalem, for sin and for uncleanness." Others speak of the gospel as "a new covenant," in the fulfillment of which God is to cleanse His people "from all their filthiness, and from *all* their idols;" and so completely to sanctify them, that when "their iniquity shall be sought for, there shall be none, and their sins, and they shall not be found." In the New Testament, Christ is affirmed to be "the power of God and the wisdom of God unto salvation to everyone that believeth," and that "the weapons of our warfare are mighty, through God, to the pulling down of strongholds."

Now the special mission of the Spirit is to take truth, in all its forms, as revealed in both Testaments, and to render it most effective for the sanctification and edification of the Church, and the salvation of men. The Spirit knows absolutely what we need for these high ends, and what forms of truth to present for the realization of them, and how to present these truths for the most perfect accomplishment of these benign purposes. Surely we ought to rise as far above Old Testament saints as the

New Testament towers above the Old. Of this fact we shall be still more deeply impressed when we have considered—

SOME OF THE HISTORIC RESULTS OF
THE BAPTISM UNDER THIS DISPENSATION

The case of the apostles. If we take the apostles as examples, and contrast their intellectual, moral, and spiritual states before and after the Pentecost, we shall probably acknowledge that such transformations of character had never occurred in the history of the world. All along, up to the crucifixion, how dull were their apprehensions, how limited and obscure their visions of truth, how feeble their faith, what cowards they were; how worldly their affections; how weak their mutual love; and how like ropes of sand were their most sacred fixed resolutions!

But how opposite in all these respects were they "*after* that the Holy Ghost came upon them." "In a moment," as it were, "in the twinkling of an eye," "they were crucified to the world, and the world to them;" and their characters took forms of glorious beauty and perfection, which rendered them "a spectacle to the world, and to angels, and to men." Their visions of truth seemed to be as cloudless as the kingdom of light. Their speech and their preaching brought the world on its knees before God. Peter, in faith, courage, and strength, became a rock. James and John vindicated their right to be called "sons of thunder." "They were all conquerors, and more than conquerors, through Him that loved them."

Power was one of the most striking characteristics of this baptism. *All* who received it "were endued with *power* from on high." Such was the power which they wielded, that the world stood in awe before them, devils fled from their presence; rulers, priests, and kings, were overcome by them. They planted the gospel in all nations. Their sound went into all the earth, and their words unto the ends of the world. They were called, "The men that turned the world upside down."

Unity of spirit was another distinctive characteristic of this baptism. Before its descent, ambition, jealousy, and disputation among themselves about who should be greatest, and even anger towards one another, often divided their hearts. Now they were all "one in Christ Jesus," and nothing could interrupt their mutual love, fellowship, and cooperation.

Boldness and courage were marked effects of this baptism. No power in Heaven or earth could induce them to "deny the Lord that bought them." They witnessed for the Lord Jesus everywhere. Their peace in God, their "assurance of hope," their "everlasting consolations," their triumphs of faith and "fulness of joy," nothing could interrupt or diminish. "They walked in the light, as God is in the light."

If we turn from the apostles and their immediate associates and converts to the *Primitive Church,* we shall find among countless thousands of its membership examples in whom the results of this baptism were equally conspicuous and striking.

For the first three or four centuries of the Christian era, the doctrine of the gift of the Spirit, *after* conversion and believing in Christ, was a great leading theme of thought and teaching. Hence there was a very general experience of this baptism during these periods.

This was the martyr age of the Church, the era, also, of her power, of her glory, and of her "victory through the blood of the Lamb and the word of His testimony." Such persecutions and fiery trials, such patience and endurance, such brotherly love, such charity to the poor and goodwill to men, such faith in Christ, such meek submission to the Divine will, such "assurance of hope," such deathless zeal, such courage, such peace in God, such "everlasting consolations" and "fulness of joy," the world never witnessed until *after* "Jesus was glorified," and "the Holy Ghost was given." "The light of the Church had come," and "the glory of the Lord had risen upon her." As a consequence, "the Gentiles came to her light, and kings to the brightness of her rising." "Her righteousness went forth as brightness, and her salvation as a lamp that burneth." No amount of suffering and torture, threatened or inflicted, could induce a denial of the faith, or draw from the sufferers any sentiments but those of goodwill towards even their judges and tormentors. "The holy martyrs of Christ," says Cyprian, "evidently show us that during this sad hour of suffering they were strangers to their own bodies; or, rather, that our Lord Himself stood by them, and familiarly conversed with them; and that, being made partakers of His grace, they made light of these temporal torments, and by one short hour delivered themselves from eternal miseries."

Take a single fact illustrative of the Spirit and manner in which believers then "endured even unto the end." At Sebastia, in Armenia, in a cold and frosty night in the depth of winter, forty martyrs, stripped of all their clothing, were placed together in a lake. As death came on, they thus conversed together: "Is the weather sharp? but Paradise is comfortable and delightful. Is the frost cold and bitter? the rest that remains is sweet and pleasant. Let us but hold out a little, and Abraham's bosom will refresh us; we shall exchange this one night for an eternal age of happiness. It is but the flesh that suffers; let us not spare it. Since we must die, let us die that we may live!"

"By reason of our strange and wonderful courage and strength" says Lactantius, "new additions are made to us; for when people see men torn to pieces with infinite variety of torments, and yet maintain a patience unconquerable, and able to tire out their tormentors, they begin to think (what the truth is) that the consent of so many, and the perseverance of dying persons, cannot be in vain; nor that patience itself, were it not from God, could hold out under such racks and tortures. Thieves and men of robust bodies are not able to bear such tearing to pieces; they groan and cry out, and are overcome with pain, because not endued with Divine patience; but our very children and women (to say nothing of men) do with silence conquer their tormentors; nor can the hottest fire force the least groan from them." So manifest did the fact become, that the places where the Christians were tortured were the holy places where the greatest numbers of converts were made, that the Roman Emperors at length prohibited all public executions of the saints of God.

Had this Divine baptism continued in the Church, long before the first thousand years of the Christian era had passed away "the kingdoms of this world would have become the kingdoms of our Lord and of His Christ."

If we leave this era of light and power, and pass through the dark ages that followed, in which this and all other vital truths of the gospel were allowed to sink into a deep eclipse, we shall find that even then God did not leave Himself without witnesses. Men and women, "full of faith and the Holy Ghost," arose in all Christian nations as "burning and shining lights," bearing their testimony to the sanctifying power of the Holy Ghost. These attained to the full "liberty of the sons of God," "walked in the light of God," and had "fellowship with the Father and with His Son Jesus Christ."

Such individuals as Thomas à Kempis, Catharine Adorna, and many others, were not only Christians, but believers who had a knowledge of the mysteries of the higher life, and who through all coming time will shine as stars of the first magnitude in the firmament of the Church. In their inward experiences, holy walk, and "power with God and with men," they had few if any superiors in preceding eras of Church history. "The unction of the Spirit" was as manifest in them as in the apostles and primitive believers. They also made their attainments in the Christian life under distinct apprehensions of the doctrines of the Spirit, as set forth in these chapters.

Look now at the state of *the Church since the Reformation.* Among Roman Catholics there have been a few, and among Protestants many, who have fully known this baptism. It is a singular fact, that while the fundamental doctrine of Protestantism was "justification by faith," the equally essential doctrine of "sanctification by faith" was first, in modern times, distinctly announced and taught within the circle of the Roman Church by such individuals as Madame Guyon and Archbishop Fénelon. It is equally true that in all the churches of every name the men and women who have been most distinguished for "power with God and with men," are the individuals who did receive the "sealing and earnest of the Spirit" after they believed. Luther, for example, Knox and his associates, "the Scotch worthies," who, with him, brought Scotland out from under the power of the "man of sin," and rendered it, for a long period, the crowning glory of Christendom, received this Divine baptism in this form, and "here was the hiding of their power."

Let us first consider *the case of Luther.* Subsequently to his conversion he had many and hard struggles after the "higher life." While studying the Epistle to the Romans, these words, "The just shall live by faith," sent new light through his soul. On a subsequent occasion, when clouds and darkness hung over his mind in regard to the subject of personal holiness, the same words, "The just shall live by faith," came again to him with new force, and filled him with the light of Heaven.

"The Pentecost" with him, however, was not yet fully come. He had heard that all who, upon their knees, would climb Pilate's staircase at Rome, would thereby attain to full salvation. While painfully creeping up from stone to stone that ascent, he suddenly heard in the depth of his soul a voice as of thunder, "The just shall live by faith." In a moment he leaped on his feet, the free man of the Lord. "Then," he says, "I felt myself born again as a new man, and I entered by an open door into the very paradise of God. From that hour I saw the precious and holy Scriptures with new eyes. I went through the whole Bible. I collected a multitude of passages, which taught me what the work of God was. Truly this text of St. Paul was to me the very gate of Heaven." Here we have the secret of Luther's subsequent courage and power. Here, too, we have one special form in which "the baptism of the Spirit" is commonly received: the opening, in new and Divine forms, of some special truth of God upon the mind, and that in connection with some particular passage of the Divine Word.

"The memoirs of *the Scotch Worthies*" disclose three central facts in their spiritual history: their conversion, followed by the common forms of Christian experience; a subsequent heart-searching, breaking up of the fountains of the great deep of the soul, and a baptism, in which they were filled with "the light of God;" and, finally, forms of the Divine life so new, and so far transcending anything before experienced, that they were utterly at loss in regard to the nature and character of their first conversion.

It was *after* this great change that they became the mighty men of God, who revolutionized that kingdom. It was no uncommon event then for one, two, and sometimes as many as five hundred souls to be converted under single discourses delivered by these men, who evinced, by their subsequent lives, that they belonged to "the people of whom God is not ashamed to be called their God." It was the eclipse of this glory that left the Scotch Church the comparatively "dead letter" which it now is.

Who is not aware that no one ever led a more laborious and comparatively fruitless life than did *Mr. Wesley before* his enduement with power by this Divine baptism, and that very few ever led a more laborious and *fruitful* life than he did *after* he received the gift of the Holy Ghost? The time of his barrenness ended, and of his amazing fruitfulness commenced, at the same moment. The same is true of his associates. The experience of these men of God should be a solemn admonition to all believers, never to go forth to their life mission and work but under "the power of the Spirit." It were as impossible to account for the marvelous results of the labors of Wesley and hi coadjutors without this baptism as to account for the extraordinary accomplishments of the apostles without it.

The Tenants—William especially—were the wonder of the age in which they lived. The secret of the influence of God that everywhere encircled them, and of their wonderful power as "ministers of the word," was the fact that "after they believed they were sealed with the Holy Spirit of promise."

On one occasion, during the interval of worship on the Sabbath, Mr. William Tenant retired to a grove nearby for private meditation and prayer. When the congregation reassembled, and their pastor did not appear, several individuals went to the grove to find him. They found him lying helpless upon the ground, under the visions of God which had there opened upon his mind. In their arms they carried him to the pulpit, where he lifted up a prayer that God would veil His power and love a little, so that he might tell the people of the "glory manifested to him." The prayer was answered, and "no man" not thus illumined "ever spake as did this man" on that occasion. Such manifestations were of common occurrence in the experience of these men, and they ever spoke and acted under their influence.

John Fletcher, of Madeley. Could any other gift of God have made him such a holy saint of the Lord Jesus; such a faithful minister of the gospel; such an effective writer in the things of salvation, whose life was so profuse with Divine influences, whose death was so magnificent, and whose posthumous power will live through all ages?

President Edwards thus describes the baptism which rendered his subsequent life so holy and powerful for good. "One day, when walking for Divine contemplation and prayer, I had a view, that for me was extraordinary, of the glory of the Son of God, as Mediator between God and man, and His wonderful, great, full, pure, and sweet grace and love, and meek and gentle condescension. This grace, that appeared so calm and sweet, appeared also great above the heavens; the Person of Christ appeared also ineffably excellent, with an excellency great enough to swallow up all thought and conception, which continued, as near as I can judge, about an hour, which kept me the greater part of the time in a flood of tears, weeping aloud. I had an ardency of soul to be, what I know not otherwise how to express, emptied and annihilated, to lie in the dust and to be filled with Christ alone, to love Him with a holy and pure love, to trust in Him, to live upon Him, and to be perfectly sanctified, and made pure with a divine and heavenly purity."

Of the lady who afterwards became his wife, and who, during her married life, often had visions of the Divine glory and love, under the power of which she would lie helpless for hours, President Edwards thus writes:—"They say there is a young lady in ——, who is beloved of that great Being who moves and rules the world, and there are certain seasons in which this great Being, in some way or other invisible, comes to her, and fills her mind with exceeding sweet delights, and that she hardly ever cares for anything, except to meditate on Him; that she expects after a while to be received up where He is, to be raised up out of this world and caught up into Heaven, being assured that He loves her too well to let her remain at a distance from Him always. There she is to dwell with Him, and to be ravished with His love and delight forever. Therefore, if you present all the world before her, with the richest of its treasures, she disregards it, and cares not for it, and is unmindful of any pain or affliction. She has a strange sweetness in her mind, and singular purity in her affections; is most just and conscientious in all her conduct, and you could not persuade her to do anything wrong or sinful if you would give her all the world, lest she should offend this great Being. She is of a wonderful sweetness, calmness, and benevolence of mind. She will sometimes go about from place to place, singing devoutly, and seems to be always full of joy and pleasure, and no one knows for what. She loves to be alone, walking in the fields and groves, and seems to have some one invisible always conversing with her."

All are aware that the savor of the writings of *Merle D'Aubigne* has been, throughout Christendom, "as ointment poured forth." What was the cause of this? Several years after his conversion, when at Kiel, in company with Rev. F. Monod, of Paris, Rev. C. Riell, of Jutland, and Klenker, Biblical Professor of the University there, in the course of their conversation upon the Scriptures, the aged Professor refused to enter into any detailed solution of difficulties presented, saying that the first step was to be "firmly settled in the grace of Christ," and that "the light which proceeds from Him will disperse all darkness." "We were studying," says D'Aubigne, "The Epistle to the Ephesians, and had got to the end of the third chapter. When we read the last two verses, 'Now unto Him that can do *exceeding abundantly* above all that we ask or think, according to the power that worketh in us,' &c., this expression fell upon my soul as a revelation from God. He can do, by His power, I said to myself, above all that we ask, above all, even, that we think, nay, EXCEEDING ABUNDANTLY above all. A full trust in Christ for the work to be done in my poor heart now filled my soul."

They then all knelt together in prayer. "When I arose," he adds, "I felt as if my wings had been 'renewed, as the wings of eagles.' All my doubts were removed, my anguish was quelled, and the Lord extended peace to me as a river. Then I could 'comprehend with all saints what is the breadth, and depth, and length, and height, and know the love of Christ, which passeth knowledge.' Then was I able to say, 'Return unto thy rest, O my soul, for the Lord hath dealt bountifully with thee.'"

About thirty or forty years ago, there died, in the city of Newark, N.J., a man of God, named *Carpenter*. At his funeral in the First Presbyterian Church in that city, it was publicly stated by one of the ministers present, that from the most careful estimate, it was fully believed that the deceased had been directly instrumental in the conversion of more than ten thousand souls. This man was a layman of very limited common-school education, and was very simple and ungrammatical in his conversation and public addresses. Before the time of his anointing, he had a mere "name to live" in the Church. As soon as he received *that* anointing, "as a prince he had power with God and with men."

At one time, for example, he with another Christian friend entered the coach to pass from Newark to New York. They found seven other individuals, all impenitent, with them in the vehicle. While on the way, or very soon after, *all* those seven individuals were hopefully converted, and that through the influence exerted during the journey. Such was the influence everywhere exerted by this "holy man of God." To a very intimate friend, a little time before his death, he made these statements: that for the previous ten years he had walked continuously under the cloudless light of the Sun of Righteousness; that the doctrine of Entire Sanctification was true; that he had been in that state during the period referred to; and that the truth would, ere long, be a leading theme in the churches.

The extraordinary power which attended the preaching of *President Finney,* during the early years of his ministry, was chiefly owing to a special baptism of the Spirit, which he received not long *after* his conversion. Hence it was that when through him "the violated law spoke out its thunders " it did seem as if we had in truth "come unto the mount that might be touched and that burned with fire, and unto blackness and darkness, and tempest, and the sound of a trumpet and the voice of words." But when he spoke of Christ then indeed did his "doctrine drop as the rain, and his speech distill as the dew, as the small rain upon the tender herb, and as the showers upon the mown grass." The reason, also, why he is bringing forth such wondrous "fruit in his old age" is, that while his whole ministry has been under "the power of the Spirit," his former baptisms have been renewed with increasing power and frequency during a few years past.

Many more instances similar to the above might be averted to, but they are sufficient to illustrate the point we had in view.

In drawing this chapter to a close, we would refer to some of the peculiarities which distinguish, and have distinguished, Christians in all churches, who have received "the baptism of the Holy Ghost."

1. One of these is a peculiar and special *savor about their lives and utterances,* which is recognized by others as unearthly and Divine. When the light comes, the glory will be seen by the Church and the world. The prophet Elisha had made but a few calls at the house of the Shunamite before she *knew* him as "a holy man of God." A very bigoted Irish Roman Catholic had occasion to board for a time in the family of a friend of ours, whose wife had for years "walked in the light of God." This man had from childhood been taught, and had believed, that "out of the Mother Church salvation is impossible." His attention, however, was soon arrested

by the peculiar spirit and sanctified conversation of that woman. He would frequently stop after meals, and continue conversations with her upon Christ, purity, and Heaven. At the close of such a conversation one day, he said, "Madam, you will get to Heaven before you die." That man was as profane and wicked as he was bigoted; yet such a character as hers could not lift its benign form before his mind without his recognizing it as unearthly and Divine, and as advancing Heavenward.

Here is a Divine something which must be possessed in order to be manifested. A preacher, for example, who is a stranger to this anointing, may be very able, exciting, and even instructive, in his discourses. But the peculiar influence which attends the unction of the Spirit only accompanies the utterances of those who "have received the Holy Ghost since they believed," and those who have received this anointing "cannot be hid." Logic, education, oratory, eloquence, physical force, all excellent in themselves, cannot take the place of the influence of the Spirit. These may have power with the understanding, but not with the conscience and the heart. This is mighty to the pulling down of strongholds which defy all other powers of men and angels.

2. All such Christians have a *peace, quietude, assurance, and fulness of joy* in God, which not only lift them above all worldly vicissitudes, but remain with them alike in all circumstances. "Their sun does not go down, neither does their moon withdraw itself. The Lord is their everlasting light, and the days of their mourning are ended." In the storm and the tempest, when "they go up by the mountains," they are consciously going nearer and nearer to Heaven, and when "they go down by the valleys," they are as consciously going down deeper and deeper into the bosom of God. "They have learned, in whatsoever state they are, therewith to be content." "They can do all things through Christ which strengtheneth them."

Madame Guyon, for proclaiming the doctrine of sanctification by faith, spent some fourteen years, as a culprit, in the prisons of France, and a large portion of these in the Bastille, with "the Man in the Iron Mask" passing daily the door of her cell. But prison walls could not shut out from her heart the light or the peace of God. In such words as the following she shadows forth her blessed experience:

> "A little bird I am,
> Shut out from fields of air,
> And in my cage I sit and sing
> To Him who placed me there;
> Well pleased a prisoner to be,
> Because my God, it pleaseth Thee.
>
> "Nought have I else to do;
> I sing the whole day long;
> And He whom most I love to please
> Doth listen to my song;
> He caught and bound my wandering wing,
> But still He bends to hear me sing
>
> "Oh! it is good to soar,
> These bolts and bars above,
> To Him whose purpose I adore,
> Whose providence I love;
> And in Thy mighty will to find
> The joy, the freedom of the mind."

Oh, when will believers generally get so near to God that "the sun shall be no more their light by day, neither for brightness shall the moon give light unto them: but the Lord shall be unto them an everlasting light, and their God their glory?"

3. *A peculiar and special form of self-control and balance of spirit* attend all who receive this baptism. We refer to that self-mastery and Divine equanimity of temper described in such statements and forms of expression as the following: "Being reviled, we bless; being persecuted, we endure it; and being defamed, we entreat;" "none of these things move me;" "I take pleasure in infirmities, in reproaches, in necessities, in persecutions, in distresses for Christ's sake; for when I am weak, then am I strong;" and "I have learned, in whatsoever state I am, therewith to be content." As the infant Jesus lay in His mother's arms, so with similar quietude, self-composure, self-control, and hopeful trust, does the soul, when filled with the Spirit, lie in the center of the sweet will of God.

"President Mahan," said a clerical friend, years ago, "I wish you could see my mother. To give you some idea of what a monument of grace she is, I would state, that in early life she was spoiled by training. She had one of the worst and most ungovernable tempers I ever knew. For years past she has been wholly confined to her bed from nervous prostration. During the early part of this period, it did seem that nobody could take care of her, or endure her continued manifestations of irritability, impatience, fretfulness, and furious anger. Right there, she became fully convinced that through grace and the baptism of the Spirit, she could have perfect rest, quietude, and self-control. She set her whole heart upon attaining that state. Such was her fervency of spirit, and earnestness in prayer, that her friends thought she would become deranged, and urged her to cease seeking and prayer. 'I die in the effort,' was her reply, 'or I obtain what I know to be in reserve for me.' At length the baptism of power came gently upon her. From that hour there has not been the slightest indication of even the remains of that temper. Her quietude and assurance have been absolute, and her sweetness of spirit 'as ointment poured forth.' It is no trouble to anyone now, but a privilege to all, to care for her. Many come, even from long distances, to listen to her Divine discourse."

Years passed on, and again we met. "What of your mother?" we asked. "Does her faith hold out?" "She is gone," was the reply. "But from the hour of that baptism to that of her death that quietude and assurance remained, and that ineffable sweetness of temper was never for a moment interrupted. I witnessed the closing scene. She died of cholera, and in the greatest conceivable agony. Yet such patience, serenity of hope, and such quiet waiting for the coming of the Lord, I hardly before deemed possible. 'My son,' she would say, 'nature has had a hard struggle; but it will be soon over, and I shall enter into the rest that remains for the people of God.'"

"This," reader, "is the victory that overcometh the world, even our faith." The feeblest among us may be "more than conquerors through Him that hath loved us." Even "at evening time there shall be light" to all who "walk in the light of God." By the grace of Christ and "the power of the Spirit" we can "rule our own spirits." "We can do all things through Christ which strengtheneth us."

Yes; there is no temper, appetite, passion, or circumstance, but this baptism can subdue into calmness, sobriety, peace, and love. ALL THINGS can be done, within the will of God, by this strength of Israel resting upon us.

4. A peculiar and special degree *of moral and spiritual power*, with God and with men, is the only other characteristic which we would present, as distinguishing those who receive this baptism. The *form* of power possessed by each is in certain respects unlike that possessed by others. Yet in all it has this one common tendency—an almost resistless influence to draw others toward God, purity, and Heaven. Some are "sons of thunder;" others are "sons of consolation." Some have special wisdom as teachers of truth; others are endued with the special power of exhortation. Some have peculiar forms of courage and faith, by which they have special power to "strengthen weak hands, and confirm feeble knees;" others have equally special forms of power in ministering to the necessities of the sick and afflicted. Others still have special power in exciting in believers the spirit of hunger and thirst for the bread and waters of life. "What do you think of Mr.——?" said one Christian to another. "I have not heard him." The clergyman referred to was a man "full of faith and of the Holy Ghost." "Well," replied the other, "if you will hear this man a few times, and not feel such a hungering and thirsting after righteousness as you never felt before, your experience will differ from mine." Others have special power in drawing sinners to repentance.

Power to *prophesy*—that is, to "speak unto men for consolation, for exhortation, and edification"—this is *universal* among all who receive this anointing. When one or more individuals in a given Church have this baptism, there will be a constant Divine influence drawing the whole body Heavenward. When the Church generally shall be endued with this power, "Gentiles will come to her light, and kings to the brightness of her rising." If, then, we would "serve God and our generation" according to His will in Christ Jesus our Lord, we must, one and all of us, tarry in the place of prayer, and struggle here with "strong crying and tears," until we are "endued with power from on high."

CHAPTER 6

The Preparation for the Baptism of the Spirit

Nevertheless I tell you the truth; It is expedient for you that I go away: for if I go not away, the Comforter will not come unto you; but if I depart, I will send Him unto you. And when He is come, He will reprove the world of sin, and of righteousness, and of judgment.—John 16:7, 8

If ye then, being evil, know how to give good gifts unto your children, how much more shall your heavenly Father give the Holy Spirit to them that ask Him?—Luke 11:13

When our Saviour came to His disciples and breathed upon them, saying, "Receive ye the Holy Ghost," He did so, not because there was any virtue in that breath, or in the mere words spoken, or because the "gift of the Spirit" was then conferred as He had promised. A considerable period intervened between the time of the events here recorded, and that of the Pentecostal baptism. These events occurred (See John 20:22) at the first meeting of Christ with His disciples after His resurrection; whereas the baptism of the Pentecost was quite forty days afterwards. What, then, was the object of our Saviour in what He then did and said? It was evidently this, to induce in their hearts that state of *waiting expectation* and *inward preparation* which are the necessary prerequisites to the reception of this all-crowning gift of God. The same object our Saviour had in view in His last promise and admonition to His disciples, "And behold I send the promise of My Father upon you;

but tarry ye in the city of Jerusalem, until ye be endued with power from on high." "And He led them out as far as to Bethany, and He lifted up His hands, and blessed them." What was said and done here, and on the occasions above referred to, created the heart preparation, described by the words, "They were all with one accord in one place." To secure the same mental and spiritual preparation for the gift to be received, was the exclusive object of the apostles in the "laying of hands" upon those who sought this blessing at Ephesus.

Had this ceremony not secured a preparatory state in the recipients, it would have been dead and useless. This baptism was then frequently received, in connection with the ordinances of water baptism, the Lord's Supper, and special prayer. Hence the Church, in her departures from the living God, retained her belief that saving efficacy was in these and kindred ordinances, irrespective of the spiritual state of the administrator or subject. From this we see the origin of *formalism*. When the Church regains her primitive faith, we have no doubt that the same Divine influence will attend the ordinances as attended them at first. When we use the religious ordinances appointed by God, in which He promises to meet His people with His special presence, with the required inward preparedness, they should be to us means of receiving the baptism of this heavenly gift. But if our faith, go no farther than the ordinances, a blight will come over our spirits in the very place where we should he "filled with the Holy Ghost." The ordinances, however, are not our present theme, but that peculiar preparation of mind and heart which is necessary to the reception of this baptism.

If we carefully examine the cases in which this anointing has been given, we shall find this important fact, that prior to its bestowment the recipient was brought into *a state of fervent desire, earnest seeking, importunate prayer, and waiting expectancy.* The mind realizes a deep inward want, "an aching void," a soul-necessity, which must be met. At the same time it is assured of an available fulness in Christ to meet this great necessity of the soul. As a consequence, there arise an intense desire and a fixed purpose of heart to seek, to pray, and to wait until the promised blessing is vouchsafed. Our Methodist brethren formerly called this state "being convicted for sanctification." O that all the membership of all the churches were thus convicted! Then would Zion "arise and shine, her light being come, and the glory of the Lord being risen upon her." In cases in which this baptism was received without being specifically expected, this prerequisite state was induced. Cornelius, for example, after his conversion, became possessed with the deep consciousness of inward necessities which God only could meet. He had also the inward persuasion that through faith in God and prayer to Him, his necessities would be met from the Divine fulness. Hence his continuous fasting and prayer. The angel of God now appeared, and gave to the suppliant these directions:—"And now send men to Joppa, and call for one Simon, whose surname is Peter; he lodgeth with one Simon, a tanner, whose house is by the seaside; he shall tell thee what thou oughtest to do." How adapted this message was to excite within him the intense desire and waiting expectation for the approaching blessing! The interval was consequently spent in heart and outward preparation for the coming of the Lord. When Peter arrived, this preparedness is thus announced by Cornelius:—"Now, therefore, are we all here present before God, to hear all things that are commanded thee of God." It is no matter of wonder that the discourse of Peter was so soon interrupted by the descent of the Holy Ghost upon the listeners, there being such an inward preparedness in his congregation for the reception of this heavenly gift. Let us now consider some facts illustrative of the subject before us.

Take the case of Moses. We have already alluded to the special baptism which he received after Israel had sinned in the matter of the golden calf. We allude to that circumstance again for the purpose of disclosing the preparatory state of mind in which he was found when the new baptism of power was received. Having secured for the people deliverance from judgments impending over them on account of their great sin; having obtained the promise that God would continue with the people as their God; having received a special communication that he was to be their leader, ruler and revelator; and being deeply impressed with the consciousness of his own inadequacy for such responsibilities, his whole being became fixed and centered in one supreme desire to obtain from God a baptism of knowledge, wisdom, and power to the full measure of his necessities. We can now read with understanding and profit the following memorable statements: "And the Lord spake unto Moses face to face, as a man speaketh unto his friend. And he turned again into the camp; but his servant Joshua, the son of Nun, a young man, departed not out of the tabernacle. And Moses said unto the Lord, See, Thou sayest unto me, Bring up this people; and Thou hast not let me know whom Thou wilt send with me. Yet Thou hast said, I know thee by name, and thou hast also found grace in my sight. Now, therefore, I pray Thee, if I have found grace in Thy sight, show me now Thy way, that I may know Thee, that I may find grace in Thy sight, and consider that this nation is Thy people. And He said, My presence shall go with thee, and I will give thee rest. And he said unto Him, If Thy presence go not with me, carry us not up hence. For wherein shall it be known here that I and Thy people have found grace in Thy sight? Is it not in that Thou goest with us? So shall we be separated, I and Thy people, from all the people that are upon the face of the earth. And the Lord said unto Moses, I will do this thing also that thou hast spoken: for thou hast found grace in My sight, and I know thee by name. And he said, I beseech Thee show me Thy glory."

One addition to this intense desire and earnest prayer was needed—a state of waiting expectation and full preparation, such as our Saviour secured in His disciples prior to the scene of the Pentecost. This state was induced by the promise and direction which followed. The promise, among other things, contained these words, "I will make all My goodness pass before thee, and will proclaim the name of the Lord before thee." Moses was then directed to hew out two tables of stone, like unto the first, "and when these were finished, to come up in the morning, unto Mount Sinai, to present himself there to God in the top of the mount." How all this tended to intensify desire, to bring the mind into a state of waiting expectation and interest, and to insure all inward and even outward preparation for the promised Divine manifestation! When that preparation was perfected, the power of the Spirit came upon him. Here we have the real meaning of the Divine declaration, "Ye shall seek Me and find Me when ye shall search for Me with all your heart." Those who do not value "the gift of the Spirit" enough thus to seek for it, will never receive, and those who know their privileges, and do not avail themselves of them, may well fear a final rejection as "reprobate silver."

We are here reminded of *the case of a little child,* in the era of the great revivals in the days of President Edwards and the Tenants, a child so young, that none expected that she would be converted. Two facts in her appearance and conduct attracted, at length, the attention of her mother—the fact that she spent most of her time alone in her bedroom, and the deep sadness upon her countenance whenever she came from that place. "What is it, my daughter," the mother inquired, "that makes you appear so sad?" "Why, mother," the child replied, "God won't come to me. I call to Him, and He won't come to me." A little time after the precious one came from her room, and with unspeakable joy upon her countenance exclaimed, "Mother, God has come. He comes to me now when I pray to Him." From that moment onward that child was "the wonder of many." In prayer especially, she had a freedom and power of utterance which old disciples could hardly equal. Nor did this distinct consciousness of the presence and light of God *ever* leave her, nor did the consequent savor of God cease to encircle her, until death, which occurred when she was upwards of sixty years of age, removed her within the veil. Reader, if God is not thus consciously present to you when you call upon Him, it is because you have not called to Him as that child did.

The case of Elisha presents an appropriate illustration of the subject before us. From the moment he became aware of the fact that he was to occupy the responsible place of being Israel's leading prophet, as successor to Elijah, he was most deeply impressed that without a full measure of the power of the Spirit that rested upon his predecessor, he would be wholly disqualified for his sacred mission. As a consequence, the reception of this baptism became to him the object of increasing intensity of desire. He was also impressed with the conviction that this anointing, if received at all, must be secured before Elijah was taken away from him. Hence his fixed determination not to be separated from him until the blessing was obtained. As the time "when the Lord would take up Elijah to Heaven by a whirlwind" drew on, the faith, and desire, and purpose of Elisha were put to the severest possible test. In three successive instances,

Elijah said to him, "Tarry here, I pray thee; for the Lord hath sent me" to such a place. To each entreaty the same answer was returned, "As the Lord liveth, and as thy soul liveth, I will not leave thee." Then they came to Jordan, where the last miracle of Elijah occurred. As they passed over, or rather through, the divided river, the following memorable scene took place: "And it came to pass, when they were gone over, that Elijah said unto Elisha, Ask what I shall do for thee, before I be taken away from thee. And Elisha said, I pray thee, let a double portion (a full measure) of thy spirit be upon me. And he said, Thou hast asked a hard thing; nevertheless, if thou see me when I am taken from thee, it shall be so unto thee; but if not, it shall not be so." (2 Kings 2) This last condition secured the intensity of desire, the waiting expectation, and heart preparedness which were necessary prerequisites for the baptism of power which Elisha sought. Had his faith wavered, had his purpose faltered, had the intensity of desire slackened, or had the required waiting expectation and watchfulness relaxed at all, "the spirit of Elijah would not have rested on Elisha." Are you thus waiting, reader, for "the sealing and earnest of the Spirit?" In due time "you will reap, if you faint not." But if you draw back, God will "have no pleasure in you."

An aged minister. Several years since we met a very aged and venerable clergyman, who asked, on our first introduction, if we did not recognize him. On receiving a negative answer, he replied that years before, while we were at Oberlin, he, being then a ruling elder in a Presbyterian Church, heard of the work of God among us there. After reading for a time the Oberlin *Evangelist*, he determined to visit us, and know for himself what was the character of the work of which he heard so much. After conversing with Brother Finney, myself, and others, he became fully convinced that God was with us of a truth, and that the baptism which we had received was in reserve for him. He accordingly set his whole soul upon the attainment of that Divine anointing, with the determination never to cease seeking and praying until he was really and truly "endued with power from on high." After searching his heart, consecrating himself to Christ, and waiting in earnest prayer, and "strong crying and tears," for the promised blessing, he entered his closet one day, under the full assurance that *then* and *there* he might "receive the Holy Ghost." He accordingly determined never to leave that place until he should receive the gift of God, after which he was seeking. He had been in the place but a little time when he seemed to himself to be sinking down into infinite depths, into the bosom of God. Here the waters of life began to rise and overflow in his heart, and to the full extent of his capabilities he knew himself to be "filled with all the fulness of God." The glory, the love of Christ, and the infinite riches of His grace now occupied his whole being. He began to tell others of the good hand of God that was upon him, "of the riches of the glory of this mystery, which is Christ in believers, the hope of glory;" and such power everywhere attended his testimony, that he was urged to take out a license to preach. As he could not do so in his own church, he obtained one from another in his vicinity. As the results of a few years' labor, more than one thousand souls were gathered into the fold of Christ. So the Lord continued to bless his labors, until his voice and strength failed. As a consequence, he was then quietly waiting the time when his Divine Master should call him to the kingdom of light. The baptism which he had at first received was often renewed, and never had been diminished, as a life-imparting power. The same anointing, reader, is for you. If you would obtain it, however, you must appreciate its value, and "seek it with all your heart, and with all your soul," and never rest, and give God no rest, until the Spirit of glory and of God rests upon you.

The circumstances in which *Paul* received, if not his first, yet a very special and abiding baptism of the Spirit, is given by himself, 2 Cor. 12:7–12. After he had commenced his ministry, he found himself greatly embarrassed in his work by some visible natural infirmity, which operated as a hindrance, and a reproach from his enemies. That such a hindrance might be removed, he sought God in prayer, thrice "beseeching Him that it might depart from him." In each instance he received the same answer: "My *grace* is sufficient for thee: for *My strength* is made perfect in weakness." As this answer was repeated, the truth sounded in the depths of his soul, that what he needed was not the removal of natural infirmities, but the grace and strength of Christ to rest upon him. From that moment the fulness of Divine grace and strength became the central life of his soul, and natural infirmities and external obstacles became objects of joy and triumph to him: for whenever these were to be encountered, then and there would the grace and power of God be vouchsafed to him in superabundant measure. "Most gladly, therefore," he exclaims, "will I rather glory in my infirmities, that the power of Christ may rest upon me. Therefore I take pleasure in infirmities, in reproaches, in necessities, in persecutions, in distresses for Christ's sake; for when I am weak, then am I strong." From that moment not only did the inward experience of Paul take a new and more triumphant direction, but his ministry took on forms of power which it did not possess before. In all his tribulations he not only himself received "everlasting consolation and good hope through grace," but was able to impart similar refreshings to all believers in all "the fiery trials" which came upon them. "Blessed be God, even the Father of our Lord Jesus Christ, the Father of mercies and the God of all comfort; who comforteth us in all our tribulations, that we may be able to comfort them which are in any trouble, by the comfort wherewith we ourselves are comforted of God." 2 Cor. 1.

It was under the influence of this specific baptism that he learned the wondrous lesson to which he refers in Phil. 4:11–13; "Not that I speak in respect of want: for I have learned, in whatsoever state I am, therewith to be content. I know both how to be abased, and I know how to abound; everywhere and in all things I am instructed both to be full and to be hungry, both to abound and to suffer need. I can do all things through Christ which strengtheneth me." We may learn two important lessons from the experience of Paul as it thus lies before us.

1. The manner in which the baptism of the Spirit is often given—viz., by the presentation of some great and essential truth of the gospel to the mind, in such form and vividness, as ever after becomes, an all-vitalizing principle in the soul, and a great central light, which renders all other forms of revealed truth equally luminous and self-imparting.

Luther tells us, for example, that from the hour when the truth embodied in the words, "The just shall live by faith," came home with such life-giving power to his mind, he "saw the precious and holy Scriptures with new eyes."

2. We may also learn from this experience of Paul to carry all difficulties which we meet with in the Divine life directly to Christ.

In that case they will be taken from us, or we shall receive such a revelation of the fulness of the Divine grace and strength of Christ, that with Paul we shall "most gladly glory in our infirmities, that the power of Christ may rest upon us."

We have before referred to Mr. Carpenter, the individual who exerted such wonderful power for the sanctification of believers and the conversion of sinners. We refer to his case again for the purpose of disclosing the state of mind in which he received such a baptism of power. He had become deeply impressed with the consciousness of moral and spiritual impotency, and of the absence of any assured hope, or settled confidence, or trust in God. He, consequently, set his whole heart upon attaining, through grace and the power of the Spirit, a permanent and settled faith, and assurance of hope, such as Abraham possessed. This became the fixed and continued theme of his thought, reading, desire, and importunate prayer. For a considerable time he gave himself and God "no rest, day nor night." At length he was drawn out into a distinct and conscious dedication of himself and family, and all his interests, to Christ. Then the baptism of power came upon him, the reason being that the conditional preparation was complied with. From that time his faith wavered not, the light of Heaven encircled him, and "he had power with God and with men."

The memory of *J. B. Taylor*, to all who knew him, and his memoir, to all who have read it, have been "as a sweet savor from God." No memoir published during the progress of the present century has been more extensively read, or has made a deeper impression upon the Church than his. His early Christian experience had the same characteristics as those of most converts—sinning and repenting, resolving and resolving, and making little or no progress. Arriving at length to the full conviction that "God has reserved some better things for us," he set his whole heart upon attaining to the "full liberty of the sons of God." The struggle and the victory which ensued he thus describes in a letter to a friend: "For some days I have been desirous to visit some friends who are distinguished for fervor of piety, and remarkable for the happiness which they enjoy in religion. It was my hope that, by associating with them, and through the help of their prayers, I might find the Lord more graciously near to my poor soul.

"My desire was that the Lord would visit me, and 'baptize me with the Holy Spirit;' my cry to Him was 'Seal my soul forever Thine;' I lifted up my heart in prayer that the blessing might descend. I felt I needed something which I did not possess. There was a void within which must be filled, or I could not be happy. My earnest desire then was, as it has been ever since—I professed religion six years before—that *all* love of the world might be destroyed, *all* selfishness should be extirpated; pride banished, unbelief removed, all idols dethroned, everything hostile to holiness and opposed to the Divine will crucified: that holiness to the Lord might be engraven in my heart, and forevermore characterize my conversation.

"My mind was led to reflect on what would be my future situation. It occurred to me, I am to be hereafter a minister of the gospel. But how shall I be able to preach in my present state of mind? I cannot—never, no, never shall I be able to do it with profit, without great overturnings in my soul. I felt that I needed that for which I was then, and for a long time had been hungering and thirsting. I desired it not for my benefit only, but for that of the Church and the world."

Such was his ardency of desire for the baptism of the Spirit, and for consequent perfect moral and spiritual purification.

In another letter to an aged Christian sister, who enjoyed all the light and privileges of the higher life, he thus writes about this time: "O my friend! I feel tired of living by the halves. God says, 'Son, give Me thine heart.' I respond, 'Oh, for an entire surrender!' Of late my soul has panted more for *complete deliverance* from remaining corruption than ever before. Oh, for perfect love! Oh, for complete sanctification in soul, body, and spirit! I beg your earnest prayers. I believe it attainable, and my soul thirsts for it; and until I possess these qualifications, I feel I shall not *be* fit to be a minister of Jesus Christ." Such was his mental state of intense desire, earnest seeking, and fervent prayer.

Let us hear the result as detailed in the letter from which the first extract was taken. "At this juncture," he says, "I was most delightfully conscious of giving up all to God. I was enabled to say, Here, Lord, take me—take my whole soul, and seal me Thine—Thine now, and Thine forever! 'If Thou wilt Thou canst make me clean.' Then there ensued such emotions as I never before experienced; all was calm and tranquil, and a solemn heaven of love possessed my whole soul. I had a witness of God's love to me, and of mine to Him. Shortly after I was dissolved in tears of love and gratitude to our blessed Lord. The name of Jesus was precious to me. 'Twas music to the ear.' 'He came as King, and took full possession of my heart,' and I was enabled to say, 'I am crucified with Christ; nevertheless I live; yet not I, but Christ liveth in me.'"

On a subsequent occasion he thus speaks of the new form of life which resulted from this baptism: "People may call this blessing what they please—faith of assurance, holiness, perfect love, sanctification; it makes no difference to me whether they give it a name or no name, it continues a blessed reality, and thanks to my heavenly Father it is my privilege to enjoy it. It is yours also, and the privilege of all." How true are the words of the prophet, *"Then shall ye seek Me, and find Me, when ye shall search for Me with all your heart!"*

The case of the Rev. A. Mahan. When "the hands of the Presbytery" had been laid upon me, and I found myself under a charge to "feed the flock of God," I soon felt myself pressed down under the consciousness of many great deficiencies, especially in respect to the sacred function of "building up believers in the most holy faith."

Under my ministry many, very many sinners were convicted, converted, and "led quite to Christ," in the matter of justification. But how after this to induce in the convert that form of the Divine life which I knew to be portrayed in the New Testament and foretold in the Old—here I felt myself "weighed in the balance and found wanting." The reason I knew to be the want of that life perfected in my own experience. Hence the subject of personal holiness became with me the great central object of thought, inquiry, reading, and prayer.

When alone with God one day in a deep forest, for example, I said distinctly and definitely to my heavenly Father that there was one thing that I desired above all else—the consciousness that my heart was pure in His sight; that if He would grant me this one blessing, I would accept of any providences that might attend me. This I said "with strong crying and tears."

In this state I came to Oberlin, as the President of that College. I had been there but a short time, when a general inquiry arose in the church after the Divine secret of holy living, and a direct appeal was made to Brother Finney and myself for specific instruction upon the subject, which induced in me an intensity of desire indescribable after that secret. Just as my whole being became centered in that one desire, the cloud lifted, and I stood in the clear sunlight of the face of God. The secret was all plain to me now, and I knew also how to lead inquirers into the King's highway.

Since that good hour "my sun has not gone down, neither has my moon withdrawn itself." Christ, reader, will never "write upon you His own new name," and give you "that new white stone, which no man knoweth but him that receiveth it," until you come to value above all price the possession of His moral image and likeness, and until you seek that image and likeness with immutable fixedness of desire and purpose. "THEN SHALL YE SEEK ME, AND FIND ME, WHEN YE SHALL SEARCH FOR ME WITH ALL YOUR HEART."

The memoirs of the Wesleys, Madame Guyon, and indeed all recorded cases of the baptism of the Spirit, present most impressive illustrations of the necessity of heart-preparation before this unspeakable gift is vouchsafed. How intense were "the hungerings and thirstings of the Wesleys after righteousness," how fervent their prayers for Divine illumination, and how teachable their spirit before "the Lord rose upon them, and His glory was seen upon them," and how did their righteousness and salvation shine forth after "the brightness of their rising!"

For a considerable period prior to her baptism, Madame Guyon was deeply impressed with the conviction that God intended for her some specific and special mission. With continuous fasting and prayer, reading and meditation, she sought to know what that mission was, and to receive "power from on high" for its fulfillment. At length the nature of that mission opened upon her mind with such distinctness and vividness, that she uttered the words aloud, "Sanctification by faith."

From that moment not a doubt rested upon her mind that to elucidate, exemplify, and proclaim this doctrine was her Heaven-given mission.

That revelation also was attended with a baptism of such "power from on high," that only a few years passed before Europe felt the influence of her godly example, spiritual utterances, and holy writings.

We must recur here to a case which came under our observation years ago, "among the annals of the poor." A woman in poor health, poor in this world's goods, pressed down with the care of a large family, with the merest "name to live" in the Church, when moving about amid her domestic cares, had these specific reflections one day pass with wonderful impressiveness through her mind: "I shall die soon and stand in the presence of God. I do not desire to meet my God there on a short or slight acquaintance. I desire to know Him fully before that time. From this moment it shall be my supreme object 'to know God, understand His way, and find grace in His sight.'"

Without relaxation of fidelity in family duty, she set her whole heart upon knowing and walking with God. When about her daily cares, she would have her Bible open upon a shelf, so that as she passed around she could stop a moment and read a passage, and then make it the subject of meditation and prayer. With the same diligence she read the most spiritual works that she could obtain. In prayer her importunity would admit of no denial.

In a short time the baptism came, and visions of God filled her whole soul. She beheld "with open face the glory of the Lord," and truly her "fellowship was with the Father and with His Son Jesus Christ." As a consequence, her character became mildly and gloriously radiant through that whole community. Even infidels, and there were numbers of them in the place, confessed that *there* was Christian character in its genuineness and perfection of beauty.

In the revival of religion which followed, none had such power with the people as she. The sisters of the Church came together and did her fall and winter sewing, that she might visit from house to house. All the cavils of infidels, Universalists, and worldlings were silenced under the power of her appeals and the Divine radiance of her character.

Her pastor, who was a man of superior education, talents, and piety, said to us, that whenever he came into the presence of that woman, he felt that he, and not she, was the learner. At the same time he never saw an individual more humble and teachable than she was. In everything which pertains to "the life of God in the soul of man," he was conscious that her vision and experience far transcended his.

Our object in giving the above illustrations has been to impress this fact on the reader, that all who receive this Divine baptism do so in consequence of a previous compliance with the conditions on which God had promised the blessing; and that without it none can fulfill his life-mission, or be duly prepared for the kingdom of glory.

Speaking of this very gift, God says that "He will yet for this be inquired of by believers, to do it for them." If we do not thus inquire, and "search for God with *all* the heart, and with *all* the soul," we shall never find Him, or receive from Him "the gift of the Holy Ghost." "If the vision tarry," and we do not "wait for it," it will never come to us.

If Christ with the Father comes to us, manifests Himself to us, and makes His abode with us, it will be because we keep His Word, prepare His way before Him in our hearts, and wait and watch for His coming as "those who watch for the morning." If our "bodies become the temples of the Holy Ghost," if God shall "dwell in us and walk in us," and care for and bless us as His "sons and daughters," it will be because His indwelling presence has with us a priceless value, and is sought as the soul's supreme portion.

Some are strangers to this baptism, because they never seek it at all. Others seek, but not "with all the heart and with all the soul." Others begin right, run well for a time, and then relinquish the pursuit. Others, still, dedicate themselves fully to Christ, as they suppose, pray for the Spirit, and then wait to experience the effect. "If the vision then tarries," they become impatient, unbelieving, despondent, and give over further seeking and effort.

This is a very common and fatal error. We are to wait in earnest seeking and prayer, *until* the promised baptism descends upon us. Look not backward, but forward, until you "behold with open face the glory of the Lord." "In due time you will reap, if you faint not."

CHAPTER 7

Miscellaneous Suggestions in Regard to This Doctrine

❋

And God, which knoweth the hearts, bare them witness, giving them the Holy Ghost, even as He did unto us; And put no difference between us and them, purifying their hearts by faith. —Acts 15:8, 9

And grieve not the holy Spirit of God, whereby ye are sealed unto the day of redemption.—Eph. 4:30

CAUTIONS TO THOSE WHO ARE SEEKING THIS BAPTISM

Individuals who set their hearts upon obtaining this anointing, not infrequently find themselves perplexed with certain difficulties and temptations, which beset their inquiries and prayers, arising from their inward experiences, and from doubts brought to their mind from without. Permit us to give certain cautions to such as are in this state.

1. Avoid forming any conceptions of the *manner* in which this baptism will come upon you, or of the peculiar experiences which you might have under its influence. Christ told His disciples that they should "receive *power*" after that "the Holy Ghost came upon them" and to "tarry in Jerusalem until they were endued with power from on high;" but of the *manner* in which the Spirit should be given, and of the *special forms* of their inward experiences and outward lives after they should be "filled with the Holy Ghost," He left them in total ignorance.

Had they, instead of spending their time in preparing their hearts, dedicating their lives, and waiting in prayer and supplication for the fulfillment of the promise, perplexed their minds with inquiries, *How* will the Spirit be given, and *what* will be the effects? we doubt whether the promise *would ever* have been realized in their experience. Let no such thoughts have place in your minds; but seek, and search, and watch, and pray, until the "Comforter is sent unto you."

Then, as you "read the precious Scriptures with new eyes," as you "behold with open face the glory of the Lord," as your faith in Christ fills you "with joy unspeakable and full of glory," and as "your fellowship is with the Father and with His Son Jesus Christ," then, and not till then, will or can you know the effect of His incoming to your souls.

2. Our second caution and admonition is this, Do not be perplexed or alarmed at your inward experiences and your emotions, especially while seeking this baptism. Individuals are often amazed and discouraged by the disclosure to their minds of internal corruption, "secret faults," and evil tendencies and habits, the existence of which they had hardly suspected. They are frequently led to doubt their conversion, and almost despair of ever being delivered from the condition of unworthiness in which they see themselves to be placed.

No such experiences should create alarm or irresolution. God is preparing His own way within you, and the glory of His manifestation will be proportioned to the thoroughness with which "the fountains of the great deep" of the soul have been previously broken up. The inward state of the soul during the preparatory process is often like the appearance of a house at the time of the annual or semi-annual cleansing. All is confusion, disorder, and dustiness, but the prudent housewife is not alarmed or perplexed at the appearance of things around her. She foresees universal order and cleanliness as the final result, and knows that everything is tending to that desired end.

For the same reason none of the experiences to which we have referred should disturb the soul seeking "the renewal of the Holy Ghost." Only let your heart be *fixed* on the "mark set before you." Put away sin as it appears, dedicate all to Christ, and seek, and watch, and pray until God shall come and make "your bodies temples of the Holy Ghost."

3. Our last caution is this: Do not be discouraged at the *time* occu-

pied in this preparatory process. The apostles and their associates waited more than forty days for "the promise of the Father." Do not give up if you have to wait through even a longer period. God in this way may prove and try you, to see whether you will or will not "seek Him with all your heart, and with all your soul," and with all "patience and perseverance." He will fulfill His promise in you, if you do not "become weary and faint in your minds" while seeking Him.

COUNSELS AND ADMONITIONS

1. Settle definitely and fully in your own minds "whether there be any Holy Ghost," any special baptism, "sealing and earnest of the Spirit," any special "enduement of power from on high," to be expected and sought by believers, and assured to them by Divine promise, after "they have believed in Christ." If God has given no such promise, it is presumption and vain in us to plead it at the throne of grace.

If God has given such a promise, and we are not fully assured of the fact, we shall seek for the blessing in a hesitating, doubting, and double-minded state, which will prevent our "receiving anything of the Lord." First of all, then, "be fully persuaded in your own minds" whether God has, in fact and form, given such a promise. When you find that He has done so—and you will thus find if you carefully and prayerfully "search the Scriptures whether these things are so," then take hold of the promise with the firm hand of faith, and plead it in earnest prayer as the unchangeable Word of God.

2. While you, in fixed purpose of heart, separate yourselves from all sin, and unreservedly dedicate yourselves to Christ, *never* for a moment after that entertain a doubt of your acceptance with God, or of your title to all the privileges of the sons of God, until you are conscious of taking that consecration back. Our faith in the promise, and our interest in it, will be weak and unsteady if we doubt of our sonship. When we thus give up sin, and accept of Christ, we have the assurance from His Word that we are, and shall be, "accepted in the Beloved."

When you are conscious of thus giving up your sins, and dedicating yourselves to Christ, reckon yourselves as children of God, and as having a direct and personal interest in all the promises. *Never* suffer your mind to doubt or halt on this question.

3. From that moment contemplate your title to the gift of the Spirit as absolute, by virtue of your faith in Christ, and sonship with God. "The promise *is* to *you*." Hold it up before your own heart, and before the throne of grace, as such. *Never* permit your assurance here to waver for a moment; you are in covenant relations with Christ, and Christ is bound to you by covenant, to "send you the Comforter, which is the Holy Ghost."

4. Finally, while you thus place yourselves as sinners, "saved by grace" within the circle of "the everlasting covenant," continue to search and inquire, and wait and pray, and pray and wait, until "the Holy Ghost shall fall upon you." Continuing thus "in prayer and supplication," "God will do exceeding abundantly above all that you ask or think." You "will be filled with the Spirit," and God will become "the everlasting light of your souls." Only be *steadfast* in faith, *enduring* in patience, and *persevering* and instant in prayer, and ere long "your light will go forth as brightness, and your salvation as a lamp that burneth."

THE DISCIPLINE OF THE SPIRIT

Individuals who receive "the sealing and earnest of the Spirit" sometimes find their inward experience not to accord, in certain important respects, with their prior anticipations. They fail to keep in mind that God is "leading them in a way which they know not," and that the Spirit cannot do for them all that they need, unless He leads them through various forms of external and internal experience. The present is preparatory to an endless future. That this preparation may be fully consummated, the Christian virtues in all their diversified forms, must be fully developed and perfected.

Each virtue takes form only under specially adapted circumstances and influences. That character may be "perfect and entire, wanting nothing," "patience must have her perfect work." Patience is the outgrowth of endurance under the pressure of heavy responsibilities, "fiery trials," and "great tribulations." It would not be wisdom or love on the part of the Spirit to free us from those "trials of faith" requisite to our perfection in the highest forms of Christian virtue.

"Everlasting consolations and good hope through grace" can come to the soul only when it is burdened with some great sorrow. The Spirit will not spare us the latter, when we must be led through it to reach the former. Victory, "through the blood of the Lamb and the word of his testimony," implies prior conflict with temptation. To prepare us for "a crown of glory which fadeth not away," and that we may stand revealed to eternity as having been "more than conquerors through Him that loved us," He will lead us to "fight the good fight of faith," to "stand in the evil day, and having done all, to stand." In short, we are to expect, under the teachings and discipline of the Spirit, just those forms of external and internal trial necessary to the development and perfection in us of all forms of Christian experience and character.

The believer is not only being fitted for immortality under the leadings of the Spirit, but is also to be employed in this life for special work in the edification of the Church and the good of the ungodly, and is constantly being prepared for the exigencies of his high and holy calling. No one can be qualified for such a work without being led through many and diverse forms of experience, both joyful and afflictive.

Paul had great perplexity and trouble through "the thorn in the flesh." That trouble, however, resulted not only in immortal benefits to him personally, but in incalculable good to the Church and the world. By means of the discipline through which he then passed he was fitted for a higher sphere of influence and usefulness than was otherwise possible to him; and by means of the Divine consolation which he received in all this discipline, he was rendered "able to comfort them who were in trouble, by means of the comfort wherewith he was comforted of God."

Every trial of faith, patiently endured, not only increases and establishes our graces, but enlarges our capacities for every good word or work. In all the different forms of discipline to which we are subjected, the Spirit leads us on to higher and higher degrees of Divine life, and into special ways of usefulness; and He will lead us through every phase of experience requisite to bring us to these ends.

We need to keep all these facts before us. Otherwise we may not only fail to "walk in the Spirit," but may quench Him also, and thus put out the Light of our souls. When we open our hearts to receive the Spirit, we give ourselves wholly up to Him, to be molded, guided and disciplined by Him, not according to our ideas, but according to His infallible knowledge of our various necessities, and according to the diverse exigencies of our sacred calling.

But while our experiences under the guidance of the Spirit may and will be, in the respects referred to, endlessly diversified, in certain other respects they will be fixed and permanent. In every "trial of faith" "patience will have her perfect work," because "as our day is so shall our strength be." In every conflict with the world, the flesh, and the powers of darkness we shall be "more than conquerors." In every furnace of affliction we shall "learn obedience from the things which we suffer." When "troubled on every side," we shall "not be distressed;" when "perplexed," we shall "not be in despair;" when "persecuted," we shall "not be forsaken;" when "cast down," we shall "not be destroyed;" when "weak, we shall be strong;" and even when "bearing about in our bodies the dying of the Lord Jesus," "the life also of Jesus will be made manifest in our bodies."

Nor will the light of God ever go out in our hearts while this baptism remains in us. Our peace in Him, our conscious sonship with Him, our acquiescence in His will, our resignation under every allotment of Providence, our quietness and assurance, our "fellowship with the Father and with His Son Jesus Christ" will never be interrupted. We shall "serve God without fear, in righteousness and holiness before Him all the days of our lives."

Nor will our experiences be without their raptures. In seasons, not few nor far between, there will be "the shoutings of a king" in the center of our hearts. "Visions will come and go." This side of the celestial city, "the glory of God will shine" in our hearts, and "the Lamb be the light thereof." "Our joy will be full." Remember, reader, "all things are possible to him that believeth." "Have faith in God," and "you shall be established."

TEMPTATIONS AND ERRORS

The Christian life as well as the worldly has its peculiar and special inward temptations, and its peculiar and special liabilities to attack from human and Satanic influences from without. Every advance into the

Divine life, from the nature and circumstances of the case, subjects the mind to forms of temptation and trial not incident to the same life in its lower developments. When the soul receives "the sealing and earnest of the Spirit," it has new and higher power than it had before, for every form and exigency of the Christian life and warfare; but is still subject to its own peculiar forms of trial and temptation.

To be prepared to meet such trials and temptations, we need to understand our state and relations when we have received the Holy Ghost. In this state, for example, we are not free from all *liability* to sin; nor are we released from the necessity of watchfulness and prayer against temptation to sin. We may quench and "grieve the Holy Spirit, whereby we are sealed unto the day of redemption." All warnings and admonitions of the New Testament indicate the truth of these statements.

Nor are we free from liability to error on subjects not essential to the purity and perfection of the Christian life. Paul and Barnabas were both "good men, full of faith and of the Holy Ghost." Yet they differed in judgment in respect to Mark, and separated in their mission on account of that difference. Both were honest, but Paul was in the wrong, and afterwards in his epistles did full justice to Mark. When on his last journey to Jerusalem, he met with disciples who admonished him, "through the Spirit," that "he should not go to Jerusalem." Yet he went, "bound in the Spirit, to Jerusalem." Nor did they, in what they said, nor he, in what he did, grieve or quench the Holy Spirit. On such subjects the Spirit does not impart infallible guidance. On a very few questions in moral philosophy and theology, Brother Finney and myself have arrived at opposite conclusions. Yet each has the same assurance as before, that the other is "full of faith and of the Holy Ghost," and never were our mutual love and esteem stronger than now. We differ just where minds under the influence of the purest integrity and the highest form of Divine illumination are liable to differ.

We may be "full of the Holy Ghost," and pressed beyond measure to utter the truths which are burning within, "as a fire shut up in our bones," and yet have need of circumspection, and be liable to error in regard to the *times* and *seasons* when we shall prophesy. To this liability the apostle refers when he gives directions how those who are under Divine illumination must conduct themselves in the Church assemblies, affirming that "the spirits of the prophets are subject to the prophets;" that "God is not the author of confusion, but of peace;" and that "all things must be done decently, and in order." Nor does the gift of the Spirit supersede the necessity of education and careful study. Timothy had received this gift; yet Paul exhorts even him to "give attendance to reading," to "meditate upon these things," and to "study to show himself approved unto God, a workman that needeth not to be ashamed, rightly dividing the word of truth." What, then, are some of the errors and temptations incident to this higher life? They are, evidently, among others, the following:—

1. *Temptation to Spiritual Pride.* Every believer who receives the gift of the Spirit becomes a new Christian, renewed in the essential elements of the inner and outer life, and has a form of life which will attract the attention of the Church and world. "His righteousness will go forth as brightness, and his salvation as a lamp that burneth." Hence the danger of making self the object of thought and conversation, and of thinking and speaking of self in the spirit of self-glorification. It is proper, and a duty, to tell others what the Lord has done for us, provided the supreme motive is not to glorify self, but to magnify the grace, and love, and saving power of Christ. When the mind begins to revolve about self as its center, it ceases, to the same extent, to revolve about Christ; and when it glories in self, it ceases to glory in the cross of Christ, and will soon be the object of Divine reprobation.

2. *Spiritual Presumption.* When the power of the Spirit comes upon us, we walk forth in "the liberty of the sons of God," and have a sovereign control over all our propensities, and all forms of temptation. In such liberty, we are liable to forget "wherein our great strength lieth," to relax in our watchfulness and prayer, and thus our hearts are exposed to "*the fiery darts of the evil one.*" When in this liberty we must ever keep in mind that "we stand by faith," and must "*not be highminded, but fear.*" We must gird ourselves with the whole panoply of God, and "watch unto prayer," if we would "stand in the evil day."

3. *Mistaking the true and proper sphere of Divine teaching and illuminating.* When the Spirit is given, and we begin to "read the precious

Scriptures with new eyes," we may be tempted to undervalue all other forms of knowledge, and to neglect study, and all proper use and cultivation of our own powers. In the whole process of the spiritual life we are "laborers together with God." Divine teaching does not supersede study and research in us, any more than our own proper activity supersedes Divine teaching.

We have known individuals who have attained to the highest forms of the higher life afterwards "make shipwreck of the faith," by assuming that they were infallibly taught all forms of revealed truth, and then bitterly denouncing as unspiritual, worldly, sensual, and devilish, all who questioned any of their nudest absurdities. We have known individuals, once deeply spiritual, by imperiously placing themselves above all need of human teaching, under the claim that they were taught of God, manifest the most proud, boastful, fanatical, and hateful spirit and character of which we can conceive.

We have known ministers of bright promise, and who were once "full of faith and of the Holy Ghost," become empty and void in their own hearts, and utterly powerless with the Church and world, and that because they relied upon Divine teaching to the neglect of study, inquiry, watching unto prayer, and the diligent use and cultivation of their own faculties. The best and safest state possible to us is to "receive the Spirit," and "walk in the Spirit." The worst and darkest state into which we can fall is to have the light of God kindled in our hearts, and then to quench it.

If you, reader, shall "receive the Spirit," and "walk in the light, as God is in the light," you will continuously "behold with open face the glory of the Lord, and be changed into the same image from glory to glory, even as by the Spirit of the Lord;" you will, as "the sons and daughters of the Lord Almighty," "stand perfect and complete in all the will of God;" every virtue, in its purest and divinest developments, will take form in your character. "Giving all diligence," you will "add to your faith, virtue; to virtue, knowledge; and to knowledge, temperance; and to temperance, patience; and to patience, godliness; and to godliness, brotherly kindness; and to brotherly kindness, charity;" and after you have finished your work of fruitfulness, goodness, and duty, "an entrance shall be ministered unto you abundantly into the everlasting kingdom of our Lord and Saviour Jesus Christ." But if at any time you shall lack these things, it will be because you have become "blind, and cannot see afar off, and have forgotten that you were cleansed from your old sins." If you continue thus blind and forgetful, "God will have no pleasure in you," and Christ will "take your part out of the Book of Life."

4. *Pride of Character* which manifests itself in an unwillingness to confess error, or sin when actually committed, is another form of temptation, against which all who attain to this higher life should be specially on their guard. With the Spirit in our hearts, we need not sin, but we may sin. We may even *"grieve"* and *"quench the Holy Spirit of God."* Should we sin, there is but one way to escape the consequences, and recover what we have lost—"repentance toward God, and faith toward our Lord Jesus Christ." Yet the reputation which we possess, and the profession we make, will present a strong temptation to cover, instead of confessing, our sins.

Let the strictest integrity always be manifested right here, and God, if we have sinned, will "restore to us the joy of His salvation, and uphold us by His free Spirit," and never "take the Holy Spirit from us." *So, when we err in judgment*—and the Spirit does not render us infallible—*let our meek humility always manifest itself in a prompt and ingenuous confession of the fact.* We shall, in such a case, never fail to "serve God unto all pleasing."

CONCLUSION

As far as *the discussion and elucidation of doctrine* are concerned, we here draw this treatise to a close. Other topics of great importance connected with the whole subject will be presented in subsequent pages. If the reader has derived as much benefit in the perusal of these chapters thus far, and from the great truth which they are designed to teach, as the author has in their preparation, he and yourself, no doubt, will have cause of mutual thanksgiving for an eternity to come. The eclipse of this great doctrine to the Church ever has been and ever will be an eclipse of her faith on the one hand, and of her vision of "the glory of God in the face of Jesus Christ" on the other.

But the unveiling of this doctrine to the faith and experience of the

Church will be to her "the brightness of her rising," to which Gentiles, and kings, and the ends of the earth shall be drawn. The movement of the sacramental host has been, hitherto with glorious exceptions, very much that of a dead march or a funeral procession. Our favorite hymns have breathed notes of sorrow and sadness, rather than notes of gladness and joy. We have made a virtue of speaking and singing of our burdens under the heavy yoke of sinful propensities, of "aching voids within"—induced by the remembrance of "peaceful hours" once enjoyed, but long since passed away, and sighings after the "blessedness we knew when first we saw the Lord." The remembrance of that early blessedness seems to present the highest Christian joy of which the mass of believers now have a conception.

Ever since that good hour when the writer "beheld with open face the glory of the Lord," he has had no form of experience answering at all to that just referred to. "The days of our mourning are ended." So will yours be, reader, when through the baptism of the Spirit you shall comprehend, as is your privilege, "what is the riches of the glory of this mystery among the Gentiles, which is Christ in you, the hope of glory." Nor is the day distant, we trust, when all Christians "will cease their mourning," and "the redeemed of the Lord shall return, and come with singing unto Zion; and everlasting joy shall be upon their head; they shall obtain gladness and joy, and sorrow and mourning shall flee away."

We all, reader, shall enter into that blessedness as soon as the way of the Lord is prepared in our hearts. If you "have not received the Holy Ghost since you believed," and have read this treatise without the conviction that such a blessing is yours by promise, then an impenetrable veil hangs between you and all the blessedness of the higher life. If the reading of this treatise has induced in your mind the conviction that you may be "sealed with the Holy Spirit of promise," and you go on your way without making the attainment of this crowning blessing of the Christian life your fixed and immutable purpose, you will, for less than "one morsel of meat," part with your birthright to "the glorious liberty of the sons of God."

If, on the other hand, you have found that "these things are so," and from this moment onward shall watch, and wait, and pray, until Christ shall "send the promise of the Father upon you," then will you also "comprehend the breadth, and length, and depth, and height, and know the love of Christ, which passeth knowledge, and be filled with all the fulness of God." You shall rejoice evermore; pray without ceasing; in everything give thanks; prove all things; hold fast that which is good; and the very God of peace shall sanctify you wholly, and your whole spirit, and soul, and body shall be preserved blameless until the coming of our Lord Jesus Christ. (1 Thess. 5:16–23)

CHAPTER 8

The Fellowship of the Spirit

And to know the love of Christ, which passeth knowledge, that ye might be filled with all the fulness of God. —Eph. 3:19

If any fellowship of the Spirit. —Phil. 2:1

The communion of the Holy Ghost be with you all. —2 Cor. 13:14

And truly our fellowship is with the Father, and with His Son Jesus Christ.—1 John 1:3

The Apostle John is the only Scripture writer whose writings have an avowed reference to his own personal observation and experience. Of Christ he speaks so far only as he hath himself "seen, and heard, and handled, of the Word of life." Of no forms of truth does he speak but of those only which he has personally "known and believed." He speaks of no degree or form of spiritual attainment or experience but such as have been fully realized in the interior of his own mind: "That which we have seen and heard declare we unto you."

The *range* over which the experience of the apostle conducts us is a very wide one. It commences with that simple form of faith which results from "seeing, hearing, and handling" Christ, as "God manifest in the flesh," and terminating in that anointing of the Spirit in which "love is made perfect," "fear is cast out," "joy is full," and "the soul's fellowship is with the Father, and with His Son Jesus Christ."

In laying before us his own experience as a believer in Christ, the apostle had in view a fourfold end—(1) that we may have, and "know that we have, eternal life;" (2) that our love, with his, "may be made perfect;" (3) that with him we may "walk in the light, as God is in the light;" and (4) that, as a final consequence, "our joy may be full." This fulness of joy all flows out of the state towards which real Christian experience, in all its forms, is tending, and in which it finds its ultimate consummation, viz., "friendship with the Father, and with His Son Jesus Christ." By sin man has lost this infinite good, and the object of the whole plan of redemption is to recover fallen humanity to this one relation to the infinite and eternal mind; and this plan is fully consummated only when God thus becomes the everlasting light of the soul. This brings us to the special object of the present chapter, which is to elucidate the great truth represented by the words, "Fellowship with the Father, and with His Son Jesus Christ," together with the kindred topics which circle round it.

We inquire, in the first place, what is the idea represented by the term "FELLOWSHIP?" Evidently, a far higher meaning is intended than mere *companionship*, the existence of two or more minds in the same locality, or the interchange of thought between such minds; or *partnership*, that is, cooperation for the promotion of common ends, and the participation of common interests, or, indeed, any form of mere external connection. All this, and far more, is signified by this term. Two minds may be connected in the most endearing external relations, as husband and wife, for example; they may often interchange thoughts with each other; they may even co-operate together for common ends, and mutually partake of common interests. Yet they may never, in the true and proper sense of the term, have fellowship one with the other. While thus related, there may be principles of opposition between them which may render each to the other the object of inward aversion.

Two minds, we will suppose, are brought together in the same locality, are associated in the pursuit of common ends, and become mutual partakers of common interests. As they interchange thoughts, each finds in the other a character, spirit, and sentiment, fully agreeable to his own. In their inter-communication there is a consequent sympathetic blending of thought with thought, feeling with feeling, and purpose with purpose; an intercommunion in which each becomes to the other, as it were, another self, making the other the beloved depository of his own mental treasures, and becoming a full participant of the other's joys and sorrows. This deep and sympathetic intercommunion of mind with mind is represented by the term "fellowship." In this relation, minds are said to "make their abode" one with the other, each finding its happy dwelling place in the heart of the other.

Notice the *conditions* in which two minds can enter into fellowship. There must be, in the first place, as a medium of fellowship, a unity of knowledge, feelings, and sentiments, in respect to some common objects of mutual interest and regard. We meet, for instance, with an individual, and find that no such medium exists between us. However genial to each other our characters and mental states may be, while this medium is wanting there can be no fellowship, no blending of mind with mind between us. Suppose this medium to be established, and that, as we come to know each other, it is found that we have no objects of common interest and regard, and. no common sympathies on any subject. Real fellowship in such a case is absolutely impossible. If, on the other hand, the objects which one regards with supreme interest, the other regards with aversion, such minds will naturally repel each other, and no blending of heart with heart can occur. But if, on a mutual acquaintanceship, it is found that there is a union of views and sympathies in regard to leading objects of thought, and each approves of the other's relations and character, their minds naturally blend in the most loving intercommunion and fellowship; and this is the idea represented by the term under consideration.

We may now state the *extent* and *limits* within which such fellowship is possible. So far as minds have common thoughts, sympathies, and experiences, so far they can have fellowship one with another. If the knowledge and experience of one extend into a sphere which the other has not entered or traversed, so far all fellowship is barred, however mutually genial their characters and experiences in other respects may be. In such cases, the fellowship of the latter may be constantly taking on new and more endearing forms, as the wider visions and experiences of the former open and expand upon his mind. In "fellowship with the Father and with His Son Jesus Christ," the soul will be eternally advancing, deeper and deeper, into "the fulness of God," as His thoughts, His emotions, His plans, and His purposes of love shall expand upon its beatific vision.

EFFECTS OF FELLOWSHIP

There is no form of blessedness so full and complete as that which results from the fellowship of pure and kindred minds, in respect to objects of spiritual and happifying mutual interest. Such a state is a primary demand of our social nature. Such is the strength of this principle within us that we can scarcely enjoy any form of good when separated from other minds. Happiness departs, and leaves us desolate and sad, when we have no kindred minds with which to sympathize. Such fellowship not only intensifies our joys, but has sovereign power to turn our deepest sorrows into the most perfect and abiding forms of gladness. Minds in fellowship become possessed to the full extent of their capacities, each of the blessedness that dwells in the heart of the other. "In fellowship with the Father and with His Son Jesus Christ," the human spirit will, to the fullest extent of its ever-growing capacities, be filled with the blessedness that dwells in the Divine mind.

The most marked peculiarity, perhaps, of such fellowship is the perpetual *assimilation of character* which thereby arises between kindred souls. When two minds are in such endearing intercommunion, the virtues and excellences of each are perpetually taking form and embodiment in the character of the other. A mind of lower, in fellowship with one of a higher order, is being perpetually raised to the conscious possession of the superior excellences of the latter. "He that walketh with wise men shall be wise." God, by bringing sanctified spirits into fellowship with Himself, will be eternally elevating them to higher and higher resemblances to His own infinite excellences, and to higher and higher fruitions of His own infinite blessedness. If we would be God-like in our character, we must seek and attain to that state in which "our fellowship shall be with the Father, and with His Son Jesus Christ."

Here the question might arise, Is such fellowship possible? Can the finite enter the fellowship with the infinite? "As the heavens are higher than the earth, so are not God's ways higher than our ways, and His thoughts than our thoughts?" How then can *we* enter into communion with God's ways and God's thoughts? "With men this is impossible; but with God all things are possible." In the text at the head of this chapter this very fellowship stands revealed as an accomplished fact: "And truly our fellowship is with the Father, and with His Son Jesus Christ." With Moses God "spake face to face, as a man speaketh with his friend." For "three hundred years Enoch walked with God." In Christ "God was manifest in the flesh," and "dwelt amongst us." God, who knows perfectly the relations between the finite and the infinite, affirms that He does thus dwell with "the humble and contrite in spirit," and that He "will dwell and walk" in such. "If a man love Me," says Christ, "he will keep My words; and My Father will love him, and We will come unto him, and make Our abode with him."

To consummate this fellowship, the Spirit is in the world, and is promised to all believers. That we may possess and enjoy this fellowship, He can and will "strengthen us with might in the inner man," and so reveal and manifest Christ and the Father unto us, that we shall enter into real and ecstatic communion with God's thoughts, purposes, and love. In elevating the creature into this Divine fellowship, God does not oppress him with the full weight of His own infinity. "No man can see the *face* of God and live." The Spirit knows how to bring, and He does bring, the soul into fellowship with those forms of Divine manifestation which it can comprehend and commune with—a fellowship which may become real in the experience of every believer, the child as well as the man.

Let us now turn our attention to the wonderful form of speech before us: "And truly our fellowship is with the Father, and with His Son Jesus Christ." We read of a strange form of love conferred upon believers, by which "we are called the sons of God." We read, also, of a brotherhood with Christ, of a co-heirship with Him, and of our being "heirs of God." Such forms of speech, however, represent merely the common privileges of all the saints in all stages of their experience. The passage before us refers to a still higher and nearer relation to God, which the believer attains when, and only when, he has "received the Holy Ghost after he has believed;" when, by means of that Divine baptism, he has been "cleansed from all unrighteousness," has "been made perfect in love," and "walks in the light as God is in the light." Then he comes into that relation with God properly represented by the term "fellowship."

You will observe that it is not said that "our fellowship is with the Father, with the Son, and with the Holy Ghost," but "with the Father, and with His Son Jesus Christ." It is not with the Spirit that the soul has direct intercommunion; but, through the Spirit, with the Father and with Christ. The Spirit, when received, does not "speak of Himself," but "takes of the things of Christ, and shows them unto us," and "shows us plainly of the Father." "Where the Spirit of the Lord is," "we behold with open face," not the Spirit, but "the glory of the Lord," "the love of Christ," and "the fulness of God." When we have received the Holy Ghost after we have believed," we comprehend what the Saviour meant when He said, "And this is life eternal, that they might *know* Thee, the only true God, and Jesus Christ whom Thou hast sent;" what God means when He says, "1 will dwell in them, and walk in them;" and what the apostle means when He says, "And truly our fellowship is with the Father, and with His Son Jesus Christ." You have read, reader, of "the communion of the Holy Ghost." Here it is: "Christ in you, the hope of glory;" "We will come to him, and make Our abode with him;" "walking with God;" "God dwelling in us, and we in Him;" and "fellowship with the Father, and with His Son Jesus Christ."

Let us see if we cannot form some apprehension, more or less distinct, of this peculiar state of Christian privilege. It will be our aim to tell all we know about it; all, we mean, that can be told in a few sentences. The work of the Spirit, as we have said, is to bring the soul into direct and immediate fellowship with God. To believe that God exists, to apprehend His attributes, and to be assured that we are the objects of His love and favor, and at the same time to contemplate Him as a Being afar off, dwelling alone in His infinity, is a state of experience beyond which thousands of Christians have not gone. To be directly conscious of Him as an immediate personal presence, encircling us with His love, "showing us His glory," and opening upon our vision an immediate apprehension of His thoughts, emotions, and purposes of grace in respect to us, and of His deep sympathy with all our joys and sorrows, cares and interests; to be conscious when we pray that we are "speaking to God face to face, as a man speaketh with his friend," and that His ear is bent tenderly towards us in all our confessions, giving of thanks, and petitions; and that all things within and around us are full of God, and that we have our dwelling place in the very center of the Divine fulness—this, certainly, is a very different relation between us and God from that above described; and all this is real in our experience when "our fellowship is with the Father." So, also, to know that Christ died for us, and that "we have redemption in His blood, even the forgiveness of our sins;" but to apprehend Him as far off, "at the right hand of God" in Heaven, and never very nigh to us, and "formed within us, the hope of glory," is the only relation to Christ in which most believers find themselves for the greater part of their lives. How much more blessed is that in which we sensibly and consciously realize a present Christ meeting and satisfying directly every susceptibility and want of our immortal natures; in which we "behold with open face His glory, and are changed into the same image from glory to glory;" in which "we comprehend the breadth, and depth, and length, and height, and know the love of Christ, which passeth knowledge;" in which Christ "comes to us, and manifests Himself unto us," reigns in us the Sovereign of all our affections and activities, and communes with us as an elder brother, strengthens us in our weaknesses, succors us in our temptations, confirms our faith, perfects our love, and teaches us the Divine lesson of deep content in every allotment of Providence. *This is fellowship with His Son Jesus Christ.* Oh, how very different is this from that realized in the first, and also in the too common developments of the Christian life!

Herein, dear reader, is "fellowship with the Father, and with His Son Jesus Christ." This is "walking with God," and "dwelling in God," and having God "walking in us, and dwelling in us." Here we blessedly know what our Saviour meant when He said, "I in them, and Thou in Me, that they may be made perfect in one;" and "I will come in unto him, and sup with him, and he with Me."

In this Divine fellowship the mind is not free from temptation. In

Christ, however, it realizes "the victory which overcometh the world." Nor is the believer free from external affliction. But in the fire and in the flood "patience has her perfect work." This end being consummated, there comes to the mind at one time a revelation of Christ in the exercise of this one virtue, patient endurance and meek submission to the will of the Father. One desire now possesses the whole being—to endure as Christ endured, and with Him, if need be, to be "made perfect through suffering." Again there opens upon the mind a vision of the eternal future: "These light afflictions, which are but for a moment, work out for us a far more exceeding and eternal weight of glory." Now the mind "glories in tribulation," while "the love of God is shed abroad in the heart by the Holy Ghost, who is given unto us."

Nor, we add again, is the mind in this state wholly, and at all periods, free from real heart sorrow. At times, if need be, it "may be in heaviness through manifold temptations," or "fiery trials." God, for wise reasons, may now and then sound the depths of the soul with some great sorrow. In such a state the mind, first of all, adjusts itself fully and perfectly to the Divine will, losing self in the heart of God, and in sweet and unreserved acquiescence consenting to do, and to endure, and to suffer *all* that God wills. "Not as I will, but as Thou wilt." "The cup which My Father giveth Me, shall I not drink it?" When "patience here has had her perfect work," the Spirit at one time opens upon the mental and spiritual vision distinct and melting apprehensions of Christ as a sufferer in Gethsemane, when climbing Calvary's mournful mountain, and upon the cross "bearing the sins of many, and making intercession for the transgressors." Here the mind forgets and loses its own sorrow in its sympathy and love for Christ in His atoning sufferings and death. To sorrow now, to "fill out the measure of Christ's sufferings," seems a privilege. At another time, in the depth of some great distress, there comes to the mind a deep assurance and sense of God's presence and love, and of the absolute security of all its interests under the Divine protection; and all this with a distinct and soul-melting consciousness of the deep and present sympathy of every Person of the Godhead with every form and degree of grief with which the heart is burdened. "Everlasting consolations, and good hope through grace," now fill and occupy the entire capacities of the soul, and "sorrow and sighing flee away."

At times, the way in which the mind is being led seems dark and gloomy. Here, the Spirit brings blessedly home to the heart such a thought as this:—

> "Christ leads *me* through no darker rooms
> Than *He* went through before."

This thought dawns in with such sweet and mellow light upon the soul, that earth's most shady places appear now as peaceful and hallowed precincts of Heaven itself. How often have you dwelt in thought upon such words as these:—

> "Jesus can make a *dying* bed
> Feel soft as downy pillows are,
> While on His breast I lean my head,
> And breathe my life out sweetly there."

Yes, reader, and Jesus can make a *living* bed, although a bed of thorns, feel equally soft and downy. Have you never, when weary with labor and care, when weighed down with the crushing burdens of vast duties, responsibilities, and perplexities, or when overshadowed with some great sorrow, had such a form of experience as this?—Jesus seemed to approach you, and to drop such words as these down into your heart, "Child, you are weary, very weary, and sorrowful. Lean your head upon My bosom, and rest there." And as you lean your head upon the bosom of His love, His rest enters into your heart. This, you say, is the beginning of that "rest that remains for the people of God." If the earnest is so peaceful, what must Heaven be?—in which "the Lamb which is in the midst of the throne shall feed them, and shall lead them unto fountains of living waters, and God shall wipe away all tears from their eyes."

With a mind in fellowship with God, there are periods of triumph when the fountains of the great deep of the soul are broken up, and when it "rejoices with joy unspeakable and full of glory." At other times, the whole spiritual being *rests* in perfect quietude and assurance, "the peace of God, which passeth all understanding, keeping the heart and mind through Christ Jesus." Then, in a state of "heaviness through manifold temptations," the soul appears "like patience on a monument smiling at grief." Again, under the baptism of "power from on high," it goes forth "strong in God, and in the power of His might," strong to do and to endure; or upon its knees in prayer, and under the outpouring of "the Spirit of grace and of supplication," "as a prince it has power with God and with men." In every state alike God is its fixed and changeless center, God its dwelling place, and God its everlasting light, while "the days of its mourning are ended." We do not think that we have overdrawn the experience of any soul whose "fellowship is with the Father, and with His Son Jesus Christ."

In making a due improvement of this subject, we would direct attention, in the first place, to an important declaration found in 1 John 1:7,— viz., "If we walk in the light, as He is in the light, we have fellowship one with another." Among worldly minds there is very little real fellowship. Selfishness is incompatible with such relations, especially in their higher and more sympathetic forms. A selfish mind sees very little in its own image, when reflected from the heart of another, to approve or delight in, or in its own mental states with which to have fellowship, such as pride, ambition, envy, covetousness, devotion to vanity, and the lusts of the flesh. Hence among such minds there is very little that can properly be called friendship.

Also among Christians who have not "received the Holy Ghost since they believed," "fellowship one with another" can obtain but in a very limited degree. In all such minds there is so much intermingling of the bad with the good, and of darkness with the light; such obscure reflections of the Divine image and glory, together with the beauties of holiness; and such meager manifestations of the Divine love; and at the same time thoughts of God and of things unseen and eternal have so seldom and unillumined a dwelling place in the heart and the mind, that it is only occasionally, and that within a very limited sphere, that there can be such sympathetic blending of thought with thought, emotion with emotion, and heart with heart, as can properly be called "fellowship." This is the exclusive reason why Christian fellowship has such a limited and feeble existence in our churches. There is among them "envying, strife, and divisions," because, for the most part, they "are carnal, and walk as men," in other words, are "mere babes in Christ." There is very little fellowship, because the basis for such experience is wanting.

When a company of believers, however, "have received the Holy Ghost since they believed," and each, under this all-renovating and all-purifying baptism, "walks in the light, as God is in the light," then, verily, they "have fellowship one with another." The reason is obvious. While perfect love banishes discord, each manifests a character that all approve and delight in, each reflects upon the others "the image and glory of Christ." Each, also has a rich inward experience, into which the hearts of the others naturally blend in sympathizing and ecstatic intercommunion. Brotherly character *manifested* is the exclusive object of brotherly love. Where the former is wanting, the latter, but in forms of general goodwill, cannot exist.

What should we think of ourselves, reader, if "our fellowship is not with the Father, and with His Son Jesus Christ?" This we reply: Such must be the state of our hearts, that moral purity cannot approach them. "The pure in heart see God," and "with the pure in heart God dwells." If God does not dwell with you, there can be but one reason for this melancholy fact. Internal impurity shuts Him out. "God never draws nigh to me when I pray to Him," said a professing Christian to us years ago. "As soon as I kneel in prayer, He seems to remove Himself to an unapproachable distance from me." "Friend," we replied, "there must be reasons of infinite weight for such relations between you and your 'Father in Heaven.' We exhort you, as you value your soul's eternity, to find out those reasons, and to put them away." A similar admonition would we present to you, reader, if God is not consciously very nigh to you when you call upon Him, if your fellowship is not "with the Father, and with His Son Jesus Christ."

To understand fully the First Epistle of John, we must recognize the two classes of believers to whom the apostle in fact, though not in form, refers, viz., those who had, and those who had not, received "the unction of the Spirit;" those who had, and those who had not, been "made perfect in love;" and, consequently, those who did, and those who did not, have "fellowship with the Father, and with His Son Jesus Christ." Of the one class he speaks as having a full knowledge, by means of their anointing, of the fulness of joy to which he refers, and as having "no need" that "anyone should teach them" upon the subject. His object in respect to the other class was to draw them into the light of God in which he was walking: "That which we have seen and heard declare we unto you, that ye may have fellowship with us." "These things write we unto you, that your joy may be full." This last is our exclusive object relative to you, reader, if you have not yet received "the anointing."

We may now understand the limits of practicable Christian attainment in this life. They extend from the beginning to a full fellowship with the apostle, in perfect love, freedom from fear and heart condemnation, and in that fulness of joy which he possessed when "walking in the light as God is in the light," and when his "fellowship was with the Father, and with His Son Jesus Christ." Nothing but unbelief in us can prevent our advancing onward and upward into the cloudless sunlight before us. The apostle has not only revealed to us the goal to which we may attain, but has made us know the way: "We have known and believed the love that God hath to us"—the love of God in "giving His Son to die for us," and also in giving "the anointing" by which we know, too, "the things that are freely given us of God." "Herein is our love made perfect." To receive, with simple trust and assurance, God's testimony to His own love to us, and to seek, "with all the heart, and with all the soul," "the unction of the Spirit," through whose illuminations and sanctifying power we may "walk in the light, as God is in the light"—this is the way to that Beulah of perfect love and fulness of joy, where "God is our everlasting light, and the days of our mourning are ended." Reader, the way is before us. Let us walk in it.

CHAPTER 9

The Unity of the Spirit

And when they had prayed, the place was shaken where they were assembled together; and they were all filled with the Holy Ghost, and they spake the word of God with boldness. —Acts 4:31

Endeavoring to keep the unity of the Spirit in the bond of peace.
—Eph. 4:3

By the phrase, "unity of the Spirit," we are to understand that form of Divine *oneness* which the Holy Spirit produces among those individuals in whose heart He dwells—that form of oneness to which our Saviour refers in those wonderful words, "I in them, and Thou in Me, that they may be made perfect in one." This unity is effected when Christ, by the Spirit, is enthroned and reigns supreme in the heart of each individual. The fact that we are required to *endeavor* to "keep the unity of the Spirit in the bond of peace," implies two things: First, that without our endeavor this unity will not be preserved; and, secondly, that this unity may exist for a certain time, and not be *perpetuated*. Sameness of spirit among any number of minds is one thing; this unity "in the bond of peace" is quite another. Many suppose that if the former obtains, the latter will result, as a matter of course, if not of necessity. This is by no means true universally. The oneness of heart and character which the Spirit creates *tends* to foster bonds of peace among the brotherhood; but, in some instances, it may, for a time at least, fail of that result from differences of opinion on important subjects—differences arising from a limitation of the human faculties, even in sanctified minds. Paul and Barnabas, for example, had both in common, as we have formerly said, "received the Holy Ghost since they had believed," and were by a special revelation from the Spirit separated to the work which for a long period they had jointly prosecuted; but a temporary separation, if not alienation, obtained between them, in consequence of a difference of opinion in respect to a question regarded in common as involving an essential principle of our holy religion.

Paul judged, that if they received Mark a second time to a companionship in the work, they would fellowship one who, by his former conduct, had proved himself untrustworthy. Barnabas judged, that in rejecting him they would deny fellowship with one who may have had good reason for the act of which Paul accused him, who was called of God to the work of the ministry, who had special qualifications for the work before them, and had been "endued with power from on high" for its prosecution. Here was a conscientious difference of opinion, and we have no reason to suppose that either quenched the Spirit in the separation which occurred between them. In the controversy, Paul was wrong, that is, misjudged, as his subsequent testimony in regard to Mark clearly evinces: "Take Mark, and bring him with thee; for he is profitable unto me for the ministry." This error in judgment, and the consequent disastrous separation from an eminent servant of Christ, was, no doubt, of great use to Paul during his subsequent life, and was unquestionably the only error of the kind that he ever fell into. To it we may refer the many exhortations to Christian forbearance with which his epistles abound, especially the exhortations in the text, "endeavoring to keep the unity of the Spirit in the bond of peace." If two inspired men, each of whom had received the Holy Ghost after believing, did differ in judgment, and did separate the one from the other, and thereby injure the cause of Christ both in and outside of the Church; and if, as Christ affirms, *visible* unity in the bonds of peace among the brotherhood is the condition on which the world will believe in Him, of what infinite moment is it that all the brotherhood in the Church should endeavor each to be one with and in Christ through the Spirit, and to be at peace among themselves. The object of the present chapter is to elucidate the great doctrine of "the unity of the Spirit in the bond of peace," and to impress upon all believers a conviction of the duty and importance of making it their study and prayerful endeavor to induce and preserve this oneness.

This unity of the Spirit of which we speak does not imply that form of sameness which excludes all peculiarities of *individual* character. Who would desire to find in our forests and parks, or on our prairies and in our gardens, an absolute likeness in every tree, plant, and flower to every other? Or would desire to see a similar sameness among all human forms and countenances? Equally unwise would it be in God to produce a similar unity in the realm of mind and Spirit. Thought would stagnate, and all mental activity come to a dead standstill in a universe thus constituted. The Divine Spirit, when He dwells in a diversity of hearts, does effect a unity in all essential particulars. This unity, however, will be like that which His creative and sustaining energy produces in the external universe—a unity in which each mind differs from the other, just as one star differs from another star in glory. Nor does the unity of the Spirit imply, among individuals in whom He dwells, an absolute sameness of thought, feeling, and judgment, on all subjects mutually deemed important. Paul and Barnabas, as we have seen, had in common received the Holy Spirit since believing, and both in common were filled with the Spirit; yet they came to opposite conclusions on a subject mutually deemed important. Here we have unity of *spirit* and opposition of *views* in an important sphere of thought and judgment. What did obtain in this case may obtain in multitudes of other cases, and thus render necessary special endeavors "to keep the unity of the Spirit in the bonds of peace." All who have the Spirit are in fundamental particulars "perfectly joined together in the same mind and in the same judgment." Other departments of thought and activity, however, God has left to the discretion of individuals. In the former relations unity, and in the latter diversity of thought and judgment, are to be anticipated. What, then, is this unity of which we are speaking?

In general, let us say that it implies that expression of oneness of thought, feeling, and sentiment on moral and spiritual subjects, which produces the highest possible forms of moral and spiritual excellence in the individual, and in the social relations of life. Character adorns itself with the loftiest attributes of beauty and perfection, when, amid a great diversity of minds, each exercises, to the fullest extent, the prerogatives of independent thought and action; at the same time all having a supreme respect for the judgment of God, and regarding it as a small matter to be judged by man's judgment, even that of the brotherhood; and meanwhile, on subjects of essential importance, all are perfectly "joined together in the same mind and in the same judgment," no diversity or opposition obtaining, but in respect to things non-essential, and this diversity and opposition creating no discord. Now this is the Divine unity which the Spirit always effects when His influence gains complete ascendancy. To be somewhat particular, this unity of the Spirit implies:—

1. A common and readily understood likeness of spirit and character to *those of Christ*. "We all, with open face, beholding as in a glass the glory of the Lord, are changed into the *same* image." Converse with any number of believers you please who "have received the Holy Ghost since they believed," and however diverse their circumstances, capacities, natural dispositions, and attainments, you will easily notice in all an essential and predominant unity in one important point—a spirit and temper, views and aims, altogether *Christ-like*. In all there will appear the same meekness and gentleness, the same patient endurance of wrong and afflictive providences, the same spirit of condescension and universal philanthropy, the same love to God and love of truth, the same purity of life and uncompromising opposition to sin in all its forms, the same unconditional subjection to the will of God, and the same implicit obedience to the law of duty, that dwelt in Christ, and beautified His life and character. In these respects there will be in all a fundamental unity or likeness, because that each takes his nature and form from a common origin and pattern which is all-powerful to conform every honest mind that submits to it as it is, to its own resemblance. Everyone who has received the Holy Ghost possesses and exhibits that Spirit in such measure and degree as to show Him to be the leading and all-controlling power of his life and character. Here we have "the unity of the Spirit" in its most important characteristics and manifestations— *a common oneness with Christ, and likeness to Him.*

2. Another peculiarity of this "unity of the Spirit" of which we speak is found in the *supreme affection and regard* that all have for Christ. All have in Christ one and the same common center, about which their thoughts, affections, and activities perpetually revolve in similar supreme love and devotion. Through Him all have a crucifixion to the world, and the world to them. In Him all have common hopes and joys, which never "make ashamed, because the love of God is shed abroad in the heart by the Holy Ghost given unto us." They alike lean upon their Beloved. The voice of each is to Him, "Draw us, and we will run after Thee; my Beloved is mine, and I am His." Ritual names, all that is human and earthly, are lost sight of in Him.

> "Names, and sects, and parties fall,
> And Christ, our Lord, is all in all."

3. A third feature of this "unity of the Spirit" is, all have in common "fellowship with the Father, and with His Son Jesus Christ:" "Christ in you, the hope of glory;" "I will dwell in them, and walk in them, and be their God, and they shall be My people;" "I in them, and Thou in Me, that they may be made perfect in one;" "We will come unto Him, and make Our abode with Him." What a Divine and blessed unity must be induced in kindred minds, all of whom have such identical inward experiences and fellowships as these!

4. The last element and characteristic of "the unity of the Spirit" to which we would refer, is this: a common and superlative *regard for the image and Spirit of Christ* in whomsoever it may exist, and from whomsoever it may be reflected. That, in character, which a truly sanctified mind esteems and values above all other things, is the image and Spirit of Christ, the beauty of holiness manifested and reflected in the inward experience and outward life. "Whosoever shall do the will of God, the same is My brother and sister, and mother." This was the Spirit of Christ, and this is the ruling spirit and leading sentiment of all in whom the Spirit of Christ dwells. It is this spirit of impartial regard for moral purity in character that lays the foundation for that Divine form of Christian practice and experience denominated Christian fellowship, or brotherly love.

We have dwelt sufficiently upon the doctrine of the unity of the Spirit to show what it is. The next thought which demands attention is that form of oneness represented by the words, "UNITY OF THE SPIRIT IN THE BOND OF PEACE."

Peace exists where harmony prevails to the exclusion of discord, and the bitterness of strife and division. "Bond of peace" implies a form of unity which not only excludes strife and discord, but resists and overcomes the strongest temptations to division and separation. Friendship is strong when neither absence nor the tongue of slander, diversity of opinion, nor seeming opposition of interest, can sunder or weaken the ties which unite loving hearts together. Take, for example, the friendship of David and Jonathan. Absence could not cool the ardor of their mutual love; nor could the tongue of envy, or rivalry of interest, sunder the bonds of peace by which their hearts were united. Christian unity and brotherly love imply friendship in the strongest form in which kindred minds can, by any possibility, be brought together. It is love, the same in kind as that which unites in one the ever blessed Persons of the sacred Trinity: "As Thou, Father, art in Me, and I in Thee; that they may be one in us;" "That they may be one, as We are one." Worldly minds may be at peace one with the other, and may be united by ties of friendship apparently tender and strong. Such bonds, however, will stand but a feeble test. Slight causes of discord will sunder completely and forever such minds one from the other. The same holds true of that form of friendship which has its basis and source in the domestic affections. Fraternal love here will seldom endure even a division of a parental estate. But brotherly love, which has its basis and source in the "unity of the Spirit," is a bond of peace that endures to eternity, and which can by no possibility be sundered but by one of two causes, or both united—a loss of Christian virtue, or an eclipse of Christian character—in which, from misunderstanding, or other reasons, sanctified minds for a time appear to each other as they are not. "The unity of the Spirit" not only induces peace among the brotherhood, but "*bonds* of peace." "The unity of the Spirit in the bond of peace" is kept when sanctified minds maintain their oneness with Christ, and have "fellowship one with another."

There is one peculiarity which distinguishes this unity from worldly friendship in all its forms. The broken ties of the latter form of love are seldom or never reunited. A friend once cooled repels all attempts at a reunion. Not so with Christian fellowship or brotherly love. Broken ties, rejoined, live when the causes of separation are fully removed, and reunited bonds of peace remain stronger than they ever existed before. The duty enjoined next claims our attention—viz., to make it our constant endeavor:

"TO KEEP THE UNITY OF THE SPIRIT IN THE BOND OF PEACE."

Obedience to this principle implies two things: that it be our constant aim and endeavor to preserve in our own hearts, and in all sanctified minds around us, "the unity of the Spirit," or the oneness with the Spirit, or the oneness with Christ before described, unalloyed and untarnished, and to perpetuate among such this unity in the bond of peace: that is, to preserve Christian character wherever it exists untarnished, and to blend and keep all Christian minds in the one accord of Christian fellowship or brotherly love. Conceive of a certain number of associated minds and hearts, each "walking in the light as God is in the light," and all "having fellowship one with another;" while it is the steady endeavor of each and all to perpetuate and cement more and more this oneness with Christ on the one hand, and this mutual fellowship on the other, while all are watchfully guarding against all causes of corruption and discord from within and without this sanctified circle. We have here the identical state intended by the apostle when he penned the words of the text. That each believer should make it his steady and prayerful endeavor to induce and perpetuate among all the members of the household of faith "the unity of the Spirit in the bond of peace," will appear evident from the following considerations:—

1. It is, in itself, the highest, the most perfect, and the most blessed state in which rational beings can exist and act. In this state, such minds not only have fellowship "one with another," but they all in common "walk with God, their fellowship being with the Father, and with His Son Jesus Christ." There is no other state conceivable so exalted, so perfect, or so blessed as that. Now, if we ought to aim to induce in ourselves, and

among the household of faith, the most perfect forms of virtue and the highest blessedness attainable, it should be our fixed and prayerful endeavor "to keep the unity of the Spirit in the bond of peace" among believers in all churches of the Redeemer.

2. The importance which Christ attaches to this state should impel every believer to use his constant and best endeavors to induce and *perpetuate* it. "By this shall all men know that ye are My disciples, if ye have love one toward another." "Neither pray I for these alone, but for them also that shall believe on Me through their word; that they all may be one: as Thou, Father, art in Me, and I in Thee, that they also may be one in us; that the world may believe that Thou hast sent Me. And the glory which Thou hast given Me, I have given them, that they may be one, even as We are one: I in them, and Thou in Me, that they may be made perfect in one; and that the world may *know* that Thou hast sent Me, and hast loved them, as Thou hast loved Me." Who, in the presence of such melting revelations, would sow discord in the household of faith? Who can avoid making it his constant endeavor to cherish and perpetuate a state, for the existence and continuance of which Christ thus intercedes with "His Father and our Father, and with His God and our God?" especially when, according to the judgment of Christ, the destiny of the world is suspended upon the existence and action of such unity among believers.

3. The *revealed example of God Himself* should be to us an all-constraining motive to influence us to the most earnest, constant, and prayerful endeavor to "keep the unity of the Spirit in the bond of peace." "Be ye, therefore, followers of God, as dear children; and walk in love, as Christ also hath loved us and given Himself for us, an offering and a sacrifice to God, for a sweet-smelling savor." "Beloved, if God so loved us, we ought also to love one another." "Hereby perceive we the love of God, because He laid down His life for us; and we ought to lay down our lives for the brethren." When a duty lies before us, upon the object of which the interests of the world are suspended, and obedience to which is urged upon us by such motives and by such an example, we surely should be prompt and tireless in its performance.

4. We urge, as another reason for the duty before us, the fact that without our watchful endeavor "the unity of the Spirit in the bond of peace" will not be kept among the brotherhood of the household of faith. Unless believers "watch unto prayer," "the serpent who beguiled Eve will corrupt their minds from the simplicity of Christ." So without their prayerful endeavor to "keep the unity of the Spirit in the bond of peace," "that old serpent the devil," will create misunderstandings, and strife, and discord in the family of Christ. A purposeless life never was, and never will be, a loving or a peaceful one. Let it, then, be our fixed and prayerful endeavor "to keep the unity of the Spirit in the bond of peace."

> "Blest be the tie that binds
> Our hearts in Christian love,"

And palsied be the tongue or the hand that shall sow discord and strife among the children of God.

5. We remark, finally, we should endeavor "to keep the unity of the Spirit in the bond of peace," because that when we cease to walk in the light, so as to have fellowship one with another, we lose all proper evidence of Christian character. "We know that we have passed from death unto life, because we love the brethren." "If any man love not his brother, whom he hath seen, how can he love God, whom he hath not seen?" "By this shall all men know that ye are My disciples, if ye have love one to another." "He that hateth his brother is a murderer, and we know that no murderer hath eternal life abiding in him." Here, then, we have a fundamental test of Christian character. "Love is of God, and he that dwelleth in love dwelleth in God and God in him." "He that loveth not, knoweth not God; for God is *love*." In the conscious exercise of brotherly love, we have the witness of the Spirit that "we are the children of God." In the absence of such love, we lose all proper evidence that we are of God. In the opposite state, we have absolute proof that we have not eternal life abiding in us. How important, then, that we endeavor "to keep the unity of the Spirit in the bond of peace."

1. In conclusion, we perceive clearly, in the light of our subject, that the duty imposed in the text has a far wider application than is commonly

supposed. The words "unity of the Spirit in the bond of peace" imply "fellowship with the Father, and with His Son Jesus Christ" in the first case, and "fellowship one with another" in the next. Universal unity in both these respects is, according to the text, to be the object of our constant endeavor. Brotherly love merely is commonly understood as referred to in this passage. The keynote of Christian fellowship or unity is a common oneness with and in Christ: "I in them, and Thou in Me, that they may be made perfect in one."

2. We see, also, how *discord* in the household of faith should be regarded. It is in itself the *root* and consummation of *all* evil, and should be so considered, and that for *two* reasons. It tends to break up fellowship with God in the *first* case, and in the *next*, eclipses the glory of the gospel of Christ before the world.

3. We are now prepared to state definitely the true and proper conditions of Christian fellowship. It is not a mere *profession* of Christian character, but the presentation of *valid evidence* of the possession of genuine Christian virtue, or oneness with God. Sin is to be tolerated nowhere, and especially not *within* the Church of Christ. If an individual professes Christianity, and yet "walks disorderly," we are *absolutely commanded* to disfellowship him. If, on the other hand, an individual gives valid evidence that he has "fellowship with the Father, and with His Son Jesus Christ," we must receive him into cordial fellowship, whatever his peculiarities in other respects may be; or we are in peril of parting company with God.

CHAPTER 10

Witness, Demonstration, and Power of the Spirit

❈

God anointed Jesus of Nazareth with the Holy Ghost and with power: who went about doing good, and healing all that were oppressed of the devil; for God was with Him. —Acts 10:38

And it is the Spirit that beareth witness, because the Spirit is truth.
—1 John 5:6

The Spirit itself beareth witness with our spirit, that we are the children of God.—Rom. 8:16

And my speech and my preaching was not with enticing words of man's wisdom, but in demonstration of the Spirit and of power.
—1 Cor. 2:4

There are certain peculiar and special forms of speech employed by the sacred writers to represent the relations of the mind to the truth of God when under the illumination of the Spirit. The word *know* is most commonly employed for such purposes. We give the following passages as examples:—"We *know* that we are of God." "And hereby we *know* that we are of the truth, and shall assure our hearts before Him." "Now we have received, not the spirit of the world, but the Spirit which is of God: that we might *know* the things that are freely given to us of God." "At that day ye shall *know* that I am in My Father, and ye in Me, and I in you."

Assurance is another form of utterance by which the same relations are expressed: "And shall *assure* our hearts before Him." So also the sacred writers speak of "the full *assurance* of hope," "the full *assurance* of faith," and of the "full *assurance* of understanding."

In the last text at the head of this chapter the apostle speaks of "the *demonstration* of the Spirit." Demonstration produces conviction which absolutely excludes doubt. No term more emphatic and powerfully expressive could possibly be employed to represent the mental results to the Christian of the *inward illumination* of the Spirit.

Those who are thus Divinely taught are denominated *spiritual*—"He that is spiritual judgeth all things: yet he himself is judged of no man." This Divinely-imparted knowledge has in it what no other has—the elements of life everlasting: "And this is life eternal, that they might *know* Thee, the only true God, and Jesus Christ, whom Thou hast sent." Let us endeavor to attain an apprehension of the forms of knowledge under consideration.

There are different forms and degrees of conviction which the mind may have in regard to a given truth. At one time a proposition may appear as *possibly*, and at another as *probably*, true. Here conviction takes on the form of belief or opinion. In other cases conviction takes on forms still higher and more positive—those of certainty, which excludes doubt. We here find ourselves within the circle of knowledge proper, and begin to affirm that we know that this and that proposition is true or false. Knowledge, in its absolute forms, is intuitive or demonstrative. Of the former kind is that in which we have a direct and immediate perception or knowledge of a given object—such as the consciousness which we have of our own existence and mental states, and of objects of direct and immediate perception in the world around us. Knowledge is demonstrative when we perceive that a given proposition not only is, but must be, true.

Here we attain to an apprehension of the character of all convictions induced by the illuminations of the Spirit. In all such cases there is a direct and inward beholding of Divine truth, followed by convictions which arise even above ordinary demonstration. In such beholdings doubt has no place. Nothing remains but absolute certainty. We "know the things which are freely given us of God." "Now the Lord is that Spirit;

and where the Spirit of the Lord is, there is liberty. But we all, with open face, beholding as in a glass the glory of the Lord, are changed into the same image from glory to glory, even as by the Spirit of the Lord."

Let us now contemplate a few facts and illustrations of the various forms of Divine teaching and illumination. You have, no doubt, reader, been subject to experiences like the following:—A given truth of God has for years, it may be, laid in the outer circle of thought. Doubt, and even unbelief, may at times have had place in your mind in regard to it; nor was it possible to render it the object of *impressive* apprehension. It lay, as a dead letter, at an infinite remove from the heart. All at once, and in a manner not at all understood, that truth makes an advance from the circle and sphere of doubt and disbelief into an open and impressive view, and we now *know* it as a Divine verity. It is a matter of inexpressible wonder now that we ever could for a moment have had a solitary doubt in respect to it, or could have regarded it with indifference. Disbelief, doubt, and indifference, on the other hand, appear infinitely absurd and criminal. No other forms of intuitive knowledge, and no demonstration, can induce such absolute and impressive conviction.

The wife of a friend of mine was passing away through the gradual advance of consumption. From childhood death had been to her mind "the *king* of terrors." During her sickness, also, she had been greatly alarmed with the idea of dying. As her husband entered the room one day, she exclaimed, with an unearthly glow upon her countenance, "My dear husband, there is nothing fearful about dying. Death has no terrors. The idea of dying is sweet to me now." From that moment she adjusted her spirit for the approaching change with all the sweet equanimity with which she had before adorned herself for the bridal hour. Indeed, the embrace of death was to her mind the bridal hour of her immortal spirit. Here we have one illustration of the effects of Divine illumination. All truth, as apprehended through the Spirit, passes from those outer spheres of thought and apprehension where disbelief and gloomy doubts prevail, and where vision is dim and unimpressive, into the inner circle of open and all-impressive vision, and of absolute knowledge. "I have *heard* of Thee by the hearing of the ear; but now mine eye *seeth* Thee."

We have special examples and illustrations of the form of illumination in the experience of converted men—that of infidels, universalists,, and moralists, especially—when under the convicting power of the Spirit. When walking in carnal security, amid the deep midnight of unbelief, impregnably fortified, as they supposed, in their opinions and beliefs, and doubly armed against all the arguments and weapons of "the truth as it is in Jesus," in a moment of deep and solemn thought, such as from time to time comes over all minds in common, the cloud is lifted, and they find themselves in the clear sunlight of truth itself. Their arguments, reasonings, and objections to the gospel appear lighter than "airy nothing"—as only so many absurdities. The evidences in favor of Christianity, on the other hand, stand out before the mind as immovable as the everlasting mountains. Such individuals cannot themselves tell how this sunlight came to them. But when it did come they found themselves at once within the sphere of absolute knowledge, the circle where doubt forever disappears.

A very intelligent gentleman in Boston, years ago, requested me to visit him. During our interview he made this statement:—"For fifty years of my life up to a few weeks since, I was a confirmed atheist. I had no idea that my belief could be shaken. As I lay upon my bed from a slight indisposition, the following reflections passed through my mind. There are in the Bible a vast number of predictions which no human foresight could have divined. Every one of these, when the time specified arrived, was fulfilled to the letter. The same Book foretells for the soul a future state of eternal retribution. These last predictions will come to pass just as all the others have done. All this came before my mind with such distinctness and force as to render doubt impossible; and I am here, a believer in Jesus."

A distinguished moralist, who had long and openly gloried in the all-sufficiency of his own self-originated righteousness, determined at one time, in conformity to a suggestion which he had heard from an evangelical pulpit, to take a careful survey of his life, write down his good deeds in one column and his bad ones in another, and then strike the balance between them. He sat down with the most undoubting assurance of finding the result immensely in his own favor. With much self-congratulation he wrote out a long catalogue of meritorious acts. But when he commenced putting down his acts of sin, one and another suggested itself, until this last catalogue far outnumbered the first. Still his sins, in appalling succession, came rushing in upon his memory. Their number appeared to be infinite. I must have forgotten many of my good deeds, he said to himself. I will run over the record of these, that others may thereby be suggested. As his eye rested upon the first set down to his own credit, that act, he said again to himself, is sinful. The *motive* which prompted it was wrong. So of every other of the same class, until his whole life stood out before his mind as "evil, and only evil, continually." Truth, under the searching power of the Spirit, having become "a discerner of the thoughts and intents of the heart," the man apprehended not only his general sinfulness, but his absolute *totality* in sin. At the same time he perceived, with equal distinctness, the infinite criminality of such a life. Now he *knew* his need of Christ, and was soon found a trembling, trusting, hoping, and believing penitent, at the foot of the cross. Throughout the whole process there was, instead of former darkness and unbelief, absolute conviction, which totally excluded doubt. Similar results obtain in the experience of all impenitent persons when under the convicting power of the Spirit. They know, as by direct and absolute intuition, their sin and ill desert, their ruin in sin, and need of the redemption of Christ.

The effects of Divine illumination, however, become still more manifest in the experience of the believer when "the Holy Ghost comes upon him." A real Christian may, for example, continue in long and painful doubt in respect to the genuineness of his conversion, and the question of his acceptance with God. Inquiry, and even prayer, tend but to dim vision and intensify doubt upon the subject. All at once he emerges from all this chilling fog into a bright spot, where more than sunlight shines upon the question about which his mind has so long hung in the agony of doubt and uncertainty. He *knows* that he "is accepted in the Beloved," and without fear hangs his eternity upon that assurance. Were he asked the question, *how* and *why* he knows this, he might be at a loss for an answer. Of the fact of his adoption, however, he has an assurance as absolute as he has of his own existence. "Behold," he exclaims, "God is my salvation; I will trust, and not be afraid. For the Lord Jehovah is my strength and my song. He also has become my salvation."

The believer reads upon the sacred page such passages as the following: "I have loved thee with an everlasting love. Therefore, with lovingkindness have I drawn thee." "As the Father hath loved Me, so have I loved you." "The hairs of your head are all numbered." "Fear not, little flock; for it is your Father's good pleasure to give you the kingdom." Such passages, as everyone knows, represent a form of love "which passeth knowledge." Yet to the unillumined mind that love is not real. God *seems* to be afar off. He does seem to love Christ, and angels, and glorified spirits. It appears, however, as if He had forgotten and forsaken me. I cannot make it real that His ear is bent toward me when I pray to Him. All at once the veil is lifted from the face of God, and with open vision we behold His glory. Nothing *seems* so real now as God's love to us and His care for us. God is love; and our dwelling place is in the fulness of that love. All that the sacred writers affirm of "the fellowship of the Spirit," of "God's dwelling in us, and we in Him," of "Christ in you, the hope of glory," of His manifesting Himself unto us, and with the Father "making His abode in us," of "the Father in Him, and He in us," and of the Father loving us even as He loves the Son, all is consciously real to the mind now. We "comprehend the length, and breadth, and depth, and height," and "know the love of Christ, which passeth knowledge." We "*know* and believe the love that God hath to us." The same holds true of Divine illumination in all its forms. When the Spirit comes, He "takes of the things of Christ, and *shows* them unto us," and "shows us *plainly* of the Father." Christ, with the Father, is to us a *real* and *manifested* personal presence, and "with open face" we "behold His glory." We receive from Christ "eyesalve, that we may see." "We read the precious Scriptures with new eyes;" and have a direct, immediate, and open vision of their great revelations. When we speak of these things, "what we have *seen* and *heard*," of these we give testimony.

We are now prepared to apprehend what is meant by *the witness of the Spirit to the truth.* There are two revealed objects to which His testimony pertains: to the truth as revealed in the Sacred Word, and to individuals in regard to the fact of their Divine adoption. That first designated is the form of testimony of which we are now to speak. "It is the Spirit that beareth witness, because the Spirit is truth," trustworthy, giving testimony only to what is true. There are various forms in which this testimony is given. The Spirit is the Author of the Bible. "The holy men of old" who wrote it "spoke as they were moved by the Holy Ghost." In giving us this revelation, we have His testimony to its truth. Doubting what is written, we "make God a liar." We have similar testimony in the stupendous Spirit-wrought miracles, and in the numberless Spirit-inspired prophecies which encircle the Sacred Word and affirm its Divine origin.

In the *nature* of the production itself, the Spirit has also given a form of testimony to the truth equally absolute and impressive. It would be no more absurd to affirm that man originated the solar system, than is the dogma that the Bible is a mere human production. "The footprints of the Creator" are as manifest here as in the organization of the universe. Through the work produced, the Spirit has given absolute testimony to the truth.

The form of testimony of all others the most impressive, however, is that which is constantly being witnessed in the interior of the mind itself when under the special influence and illumination of the Spirit. We call a physician, who prescribes a certain medicine, and at the same time designates certain specific effects which will follow its administration. In the experience of those identical results, we have proof of that physician's knowledge and integrity. The Scriptures map out beforehand endlessly diversified forms of experience and character, as resulting from our believing and obeying the gospel. As these experiences follow our faith and obedience—all in exact accordance with "what is written"—and as these results do and can follow under no other influences, we know, and cannot but know, that "the Spirit is truth." As these results are Divine in their nature, we also know that the truth which induces them must, through the Spirit, "come down from the Father of lights." The "everlasting consolations," the immortal hopes, the Divine fellowships, the moral virtues, and the fulness of joy, all consciously received through a superhuman and Divine influence, are so many witnesses within, that we are being led, and taught, and filled by "the Spirit of the living God." "We have the witness in ourselves."

"The Spirit," we are also told, "beareth witness with our spirit that we are the children of God." How is this testimony borne? Of this we are, in one particular, informed in the context. "For as many as are led by the Spirit of God, they are the sons of God. For ye have not received the spirit of bondage again to fear; but ye have received the Spirit of adoption, whereby we cry, Abba, Father." The apostle then adds: "The Spirit beareth witness with"—that is, in connection with or through—"our spirit"—the spirit of adoption which He induces in us—"that we are the children of God." In the exercise of the spirit of adoption, we recognize God as our Father, and ourselves as His children. In effecting this spirit within us, the Holy Ghost superadds His testimony to the fact that we are God's sons and daughters. If we were not such, the Holy Ghost would not create the spirit of sonship in our hearts.

The believer, as he advances onward "in the light of God"—and we always walk in that light when we have the Spirit—receives at length an absolute inward *assurance* of His Divine adoption. From that moment "he knows that he is of God," and can no more doubt it than he can cease to be conscious of his own being. In giving us that assurance, the Spirit gives us with it His testimony that "we are children of God," and we distinctly recognize His testimony to that fact.

The believer often passes through a form of experience in which "patience has her perfect work," and in which "tribulation worketh patience, and patience, experience; and experience, hope; and hope maketh not ashamed, because the love of God is shed abroad in our hearts by the Holy Ghost which is given unto us." When the Spirit thus "sheds abroad" that love, He gives with it His absolute testimony to the fact that "we are the children of God." In conducting us through such hallowed experiences, He testifies to and with our spirit that God is dealing with us "as with sons," disciplining us "for our profit, that we may be partakers of His holiness."

So, when "the Spirit helpeth our infirmities," we, "not knowing what we should pray for as we ought," "He maketh intercession for us according to the will of God;" and thus influenced and directed, we "ask and receive" "until our joy is full." In inducing these filial and parental relations between us and God, the Spirit, in the most absolute form conceivable, "testifies with our spirit that we are the children of God."

During the era of deadly persecution in Scotland, when "the baptism of the Spirit" was the common experience of believers, and the myrmidons of the persecuting power were marauding the whole country to murder the saints and break up the religious assemblies, a young woman, on her way to such a meeting, was met by a company of cavalry, and required to give her destination. She could not "deny the faith," and would not reveal the place of meeting. At that moment this promise presented itself to her mind: "It shall be given you in that same hour what ye shall speak." She lifted a secret prayer that God would then give her what she should speak. Instantly these words presented themselves, and she uttered them as presented: "I am going to my Father's house. My elder Brother has died. His will is to be read today, and I have an interest in it." The commander bid her go on her way. "I hope," he added, "you will find a rich portion left to yourself." Could the Spirit have given that young saint any more absolute testimony that she was a child of God?

At that same era, two brethren were helping their loved pastor, who was crippled with rheumatism, on to such a meeting. On their way, they discovered a troop of those murderers approaching. As they could not in time carry their pastor to a place of safety, he entreated them to leave him, and save themselves. They replied that they should stay and die with him. As they would not be persuaded, he lifted a prayer that God would interpose, and conceal them from their persecutors. Instantly a thick cloud came over the top of the mountain, and covered them, so their murderers passed close by their victims without seeing them at all. Did those individuals need from the Spirit any other testimony that they were "the children of God?" Every answer we receive to prayer is a testimony of the same kind.

We remark once more, when the Spirit brings us into conscious "fellowship with the Father, and with His Son Jesus Christ;" when He enables us to "know the love of Christ, which passeth knowledge," and "fills us with all the fulness of God;" when we "behold with open face the glory of the Lord," and are "changed into the same image from glory to glory, even as by the Spirit of the Lord;" and when, by His indwelling presence and illumination, "God becomes our everlasting light, and the days of our mourning are ended"—in all this we have the absolute testimony of the Spirit to our adoption. We need, as Mr. Wesley says, no voice without, and no words within, to know that we have this witness. What we do need is, "full assurance of hope," "full assurance of faith," and "full assurance of understanding." These the Spirit gives us; and in these we have His testimony that "we are the children of God."

Truth in all its forms, when apprehended through the Spirit, has not only an all-illuminating and all-convincing, but equally an *all-vitalizing power*—a power to quicken into the highest possible activity every faculty and susceptibility of our nature. Every truth of God, and at the same time all that we are capable of being and becoming through Divine influence, lie out with perfect distinctness under the eye of the Spirit. At each successive moment, therefore, He is able, we co-working with Him, to produce in us those specific apprehensions, desires, and purposes, which will render our activity the most perfect, our blessedness the most full, and our virtues the most Divine. Nothing possible to our natures lies beyond His power to induce in us, and to enable us to accomplish. He knows us as we do not and cannot know ourselves; and not what we know of ourselves, but what He knows us as capable of being, becoming, doing, and enjoying, is the limit and measure of His power to do in and through us.

As "laborers together with God" for His kingdom and glory, the Spirit knows how to produce in us just those apprehensions of God, Christ, life, death, duty, redemption, eternity, and retribution, just those emotions, desires, purposes, forms of utterance, and modes of action, which will render our agency the most efficient for the purposes of our "high calling of God in Christ Jesus." Yes, reader, God by His Spirit is "able to make all grace abound toward you, that you, always having all sufficiency in all things, may abound unto every good work." Girded by the power of the Spirit, the weakest among us may do valiant service "for the great Captain of our salvation." The same Almighty power which the Spirit "wrought in Christ, when He raised Him from the dead, and set Him at the right hand of God in the heavenly places, far above all principality, and power, and might, and dominion, and every name that is named, not only in this world, but in that which is to come," we are absolutely assured, is equally mighty to usward in reference to all our spiritual necessities and exigencies; yes, equally mighty to do in and for us "exceeding abundantly above all that we ask or think." Nothing can exceed the impressiveness of the language of the apostle upon this subject, viz.,

"Wherefore I also, after I heard of your faith in the Lord Jesus, and love unto all the saints, cease not to give thanks for you, making mention of you in my prayers; that the God of our Lord Jesus Christ, the Father of glory, may give unto you the spirit of wisdom and revelation in the knowledge of Him: the eyes of your understanding being enlightened; that ye may know what is the hope of His calling, and what the riches of the glory of His inheritance in the saints, and what is the exceeding greatness of His power to usward who believe, according to the working of His mighty power, which He wrought in Christ, when He raised *Him* from the dead, and set Him at His own right hand in the heavenly *places,* far above all principality, and power, and might, and dominion, and every name that is named, not only in this world, but also in that which is to come: and hath put all *things* under His feet, and gave Him *to be* the Head over all *things* to the Church, which is His body, the fulness of Him that filleth all in all."

There are two distinct and opposite states and relations in which the believer in Jesus may be contemplated. In the one state he has repented of sin, "believed to the saving of his soul," entertains sincere purposes of obedience, and is not *utterly* barren of good works. In the other state he has all these, with "the power of the Spirit" superadded. As a necessary consequence, a fundamental difference arises in the forms which Christian experience and action take on. In the former state the leading characteristics of such experience are imbecility, inward emptiness, and want; doing what we would not, and not doing what we would; a perpetual "laying again the foundation of repentance from dead works to serve the living God;" intervals of light, with longer continued periods of darkness and gloom; periods of hope and assurance, but more of doubt and fear; occasional joys, "but much of sorrow, much of woe;" much of crying after God, but very little, if any "communion of the Spirit;" and many fightings, but very few "victories by the blood of the Lamb and the word of His testimony." In the latter state the equally marked characteristics of that experience are courage and strength; "everlasting consolations and good hope through grace;" "victories by the blood of the Lamb and the word of His testimony;" "the light of God, and with it full assurance of faith," "full assurance of hope," and "full assurance of understanding;" "all-sufficiency in all things," and thereby "abounding unto every good work;" immortal fellowships and "fulness of joy;" and God as our "everlasting light," while "the days of our mourning are ended."

"The Church of the living God" should ever be in that state in which "he that is feeble among us is as David, and the house of David as God, as the angel of the Lord before Him." On what conditions can we be girded with this everlasting strength? We must, in the first place, fully appreciate our own weaknesses and insufficiency in ourselves, and utterly and forever renounce and repudiate the principle of self-sufficiency and dependence. "We are not sufficient of ourselves to think anything as of ourselves." This truth must be omnipresent in our mind. In the next place, we must as fully appreciate the *available* strength which exists for us in God. "Our sufficiency is of God," and in Him we have "all-sufficiency for all things." We "can do all things through Christ, who strengtheneth us." In our assurance of *available* "strength in the Lord, and in the power of His might," we must never waver. Lastly, our hope and our trust must be, "not in ourselves, but in God." "If we will not believe, we shall not be established." If we do believe, our "light will go forth as brightness, and our salvation as a lamp that shineth." At all times and in every exigency "the grace of Christ will be sufficient for us." Here lies the grand secret of holy living. "Have faith in God." "We believe, and therefore speak." "If thou canst believe: all things are possible to him that believeth." Self-distrust and "faith in God." Here is the Divine secret, which "none of the wicked," and too few believers "understand;" but which the "wise do understand." May you, reader, know this Divine secret!

As far as "the full assurance of faith," "the full assurance of hope," "the full assurance of understanding," and that form of fear which is "cast out by perfect love," are concerned, fear should have no place whatever in Christian experience. All in common should "serve God without fear, in righteousness and holiness before Him, *all* the days of their lives." Yet there are certain possibilities and perils attendant on the Christian life which should induce that sober vigilance and wakeful circumspection and watchfulness, represented by the words "godly fear" and "fear and trembling." Notwithstanding the availability, the all-sufficiency of Divine grace, and "the power of the Spirit," we may "cast away our confidence," "sell our birthright," "quench the Spirit," and be "corrupted from the simplicity that is in Christ." The immutable condition of final salvation with us is, that we "hold the beginning of our confidence steadfast, even unto the end." For the want of proper diligence in "stirring the gift of God which is in us," the gift of the Spirit, we may fail to glorify God by "bearing much fruit." We must "keep our bodies under, and bring them into subjection," or ourselves be "castaways." In every department of the Christian life and work, we are "laborers together with God," and encircled with adversaries ever wakeful, watchful, and of mighty power. Such considerations, while they should not dim our hopes, weaken our assurances, or lessen our fulness of joy, should render us "sober-minded" and "watchful unto prayer." "There is no time for trifling here," for anything but sober-minded circumspection. If we will be thus "sober and vigilant," Christ through the Spirit will "make all grace *abound* toward us," so that we shall "always have all-sufficiency in *all* things." But "if we will not watch, Christ will come upon us as a thief," and "remove our candlestick out of its place."

CHAPTER 11

The Fountain Opened for Sin and for Uncleanness, or The Cleansing Power of the Spirit

❊

But of Him are ye in Christ Jesus, who of God is made unto us wisdom, and righteousness, and sanctification, and redemption.
—1 Cor. 1:30

In that day there shall be a fountain opened to the house of David and to the inhabitants of Jerusalem for sin and for uncleanness.
—Zech. 13:1

Not by works of righteousness which we have done, but according to His mercy He saved us, by the washing of regeneration, and renewing of the Holy Ghost. —Titus 3:5

In Palestine and surrounding countries, the people, in ages past, were sometimes in great peril from want of water, occasioned by either of two circumstances—drought, or the besieging of cities, when the usual supply was cut off by encircling foes. Hence it was that the greatest pains were then taken by the inhabitants exposed to such evils, to provide against them.

The method generally adopted was to dig out in the solid rock beneath the surface on which such cities were built, vast reservoirs, which, in periods of rain, were filled with water and then sealed up, so as to be preserved pure until times of extremity should come. Then they were opened to quench thirst, and for external cleansing.

In searching amid the ruins of such cities, vast rows of such fountains or reservoirs have been found. Some of these fountains are from one to three hundred feet deep, and as many in diameter. When a city was well furnished with such sealed fountains, they would be to all the inhabitants a source of great blessedness, because they would see in them abundant security against evils which were certain to impend at some time.

When the ordinary supply of water was cut off for either of the reasons assigned, then all minds would be turned with intense desire to the sealed fountains within the city, and the opening of the same would be the object of one common, all-pervading prayer to the public authorities, to whose control such fountains were subject. While the keeping of those fountains closed at such times would be the occasion of general sorrow and regret, the opening of them would be as the first note of the trump of jubilee to the people. Such an event brought deliverance from two forms of death—thirst within, and uncleanness breeding pestilence, without.

Sometimes, when the fountains were opened, it would be found, to the amazement and horror of the expectant multitude, that through some fissures in the rocks the waters had escaped, and the fountains were dry. These were the "broken cisterns," or fountains "that could hold no water." Hence it is that these fountains afford some of the most beautiful and impressive figures found in the Scriptures. When, for example, a person was to an individual a source and cause of great serenity, peace, and consolation, and at the same time the object of most endeared affection, the former would be said to be to the latter "a fountain sealed;" "a fountain sealed is My beloved unto Me."

When individuals were subject, from any cause, to very great joy and triumph, or to great deliverances from impending dangers, the cause of such joy and deliverance was compared to a fountain opened during the straits of drought or of siege, "Thou wilt open unto him the fountains of life."

As in the land of oppressive heat, the water, cool and fresh, welling up from the heart of the earth, was, in itself, more refreshing than the rainwater drawn from the hewn-rock fountains, invaluable as the latter was in times of extremity, so when an object was to the mind the source and cause of the greatest conceivable good, it was compared to "a fountain of living water." On the other hand, when an object had been the source and cause of the highest hope, and had flagrantly wrecked and disappointed that hope, it was compared to a "broken cistern," a fountain opened in time of pressing necessity, and to the horror of the expectant multitude found empty.

When an individual was seen abandoning that which would be to him the source of the greatest good, and pursuing with eager haste that which would be to him the cause of certain ruin and death, he was compared to one who "forsakes a fountain of living water, and hews out to himself a broken cistern that can hold no water;" as if a man should refuse to taste of living water welling up from a perennial spring near him, and was seen laboriously striving to hew out for himself, in a visibly shelly and split rock, a cistern, to receive the rainwater that might run into it from the clouds above.

We may now apply the impressive figure in which the redemption of Christ is set before us in the text, together with the attitude of the heart of the Church in respect to that redemption, as the latter-day glory dawns in. The text, you will bear in mind, sets before us, in one and the same figure, the salvation of Christ, in what may be called its objective and subjective relations—that is, salvation as it is in itself, and the state of the heart relatively to it, when Christ becomes "the power of God and the wisdom of God unto the believer."

In itself, whether men avail themselves of it or not, that salvation is "perfect and entire, wanting nothing." It contains and reveals provisions, full and complete, for all the moral and spiritual necessities of the soul. These provisions, however, only become efficacious to this end when the soul, supremely desirous to be wholly free from the condemnation, power, and inbeing of sin, sees in Christ a sovereign remedy for this death-plague, and comes to Him, and trusts in the virtue of His blood as the "fountain opened for sin and for uncleanness."

Think of the inhabitants of an Eastern city in a time of extreme droughts, when the living fountains and wells within and around are completely dried; or in the straitness of a siege, when all watercourses are stopped, or turned aside by the encircling foe. In this state, everyone is perishing with a burning thirst, and terror-stricken with the apprehension of the all-pervading presence of the death-plague from uncleanness.

In the sealed fountains within the city is the only sovereign remedy for both these forms of impending death. One desire now pervades all minds, and one prayer goes up to the ruling authorities. It is, that these fountains may be opened to save the people from these terrible calamities. When the fountains are opened, what a universal rush there is to them, to obtain those waters of life! and with what eagerness are they applied to quench the burning thirst, and cleanse away the external impurity!

Such is the state of the heart relatively to the provisions of saving grace in Christ, when they become efficacious for the pardon of sin, and for moral and spiritual purification. When the mind is divided by the attractions of things seen and temporal, and drawn by "the lust of the flesh, and the lust of the eyes, and the pride of life," away from God, and holiness, and Heaven; when self-righteousness or unbelief closes the avenues of the heart to Christ and the Spirit of grace—then these provisions in Christ have no more efficacy for the salvation of the soul than if they had no existence at all. Christ is then to the soul, not a "fountain *opened* for sin and for uncleanness," but a fountain *closed*.

When preached by the Holy Ghost, Christ was "to the Jew a stumbling block, and to the Greek foolishness," because the "Jew sought for a sign, and the Greek for wisdom." That is, each held in supreme regard something incompatible with the outgoing of the heart in a supreme desire and choice towards Christ and His salvation. But to everyone that believeth, He was, and He is, "the power of God and the wisdom of God unto salvation," because all such appreciate the infinite value of His grace, and seek it in Him with all the heart and with all the soul.

Such is the salvation of Christ in its subjective and objective relations, as it is in itself closed, and as it is unsealed to the believing heart—"a fountain opened for sin and uncleanness." When Christ is formed within the soul, the hope of glory, and with perfect quietness and assurance reposes in Him for all future necessities, receiving everlasting consolation and peace through His grace, then He is to such a "fountain of living waters."

When one predominant desire possesses the mind, to be wholly free from the condemnation and power of sin, and in perfect purity to be "filled with all the fulness of God;" and when in Christ it apprehends a present and perfect sufficiency to meet all its desires and necessities, then Christ is to the soul "a fountain opened for sin and for uncleanness." The soul realizes the blessings of a present Christ immediately, fully, and specifically flowing into every susceptibility and want of its immortal nature.

It is to a state of hunger and thirst for righteousness, to an inward panting and crying out of the whole inner being for God and the light of His countenance, that the "exceeding great and precious promises" are addressed, by which we become "partakers of the Divine nature."

When all the powers of the soul are preoccupied and filled with worldly attachments incompatible with the indwelling of the Holy Ghost; when worldly pride, the spirit of self-righteousness and unbelief, repel the approach of the doctrine of Christ crucified for our redemption; the individual who reasons with him upon righteousness, temperance, and a judgment to come, and commends to him the full salvation in Christ "for sin and for uncleanness," is to him as a mocker or one that brings strange things to his ears.

In our cities are various reservoirs, the contents of which are in reserve in case of fire. What if the authorities should open these, and invite the people to use them for quenching their thirst and for external purification. You would regard your rulers as demented. Your wells and your cisterns are filled with living or pure cloud water. You have no liking for the filthy water in the reservoirs referred to, and you would condemn as an insult an invitation to partake of them.

With somewhat similar feelings do men who think they have all and abound, regard the provisions of grace for their redemption. They esteem it quite meritorious if, for once a week, when convenience serves, they attend upon the services of the sanctuary, where these provisions are urged upon their acceptance; while the majority of men contemn even so much regard for sacred things as that.

But suppose God should send a drought in which all moisture should be burnt out of the earth beneath and the atmosphere above and around you. Your wells and cisterns and rivers are dried up, and your lakes even have become stagnant pools of death-poison. One want presses upon the people—water. Even the street water in your reservoirs would then be regarded as of priceless value.

But suppose that the public authorities should now open sealed fountains, filled with the pure liquid which the clouds and dews of Heaven had rained down among you. How would you then regard the cry, "Ho! everyone that thirsteth come ye to the waters!" With similar feelings do men regard the provisions of life in Christ, when they become conscious of their real condition as sinners; and it is, we repeat, to this poverty of spirit, this inward cry for the waters of life in Christ, that the invitations and promises of Christ are addressed.

We now advance to a very important inquiry—viz., what are we to understand by the declaration, "*In that day* there shall be a fountain opened to the house of David, and to the inhabitants of Jerusalem, for sin and for uncleanness?" The text implies that the time is coming when the Church is to attain to a new form of experience in Christ, not common, and by no means general in any preceding age. "In *that day* there shall be a fountain opened." There is great meaning in these memorable words "that day."

Let us inquire for the meaning of this prophecy. Christ in Himself, and in the fulness, completeness, and efficacy of the provisions of grace in Him for all the wants of the soul, "is the same yesterday, and today, and forever." "Ye are complete in Him," will hold equally true of the Church, as far as Christ's power to save is concerned, at any one moment from the beginning to the end of time, as at any other. In consequence of a change of relations of the heart of the Church, however, He may be to her in degree and in fulness a Saviour such as He had never before been.

Such a change did occur in the experience of the disciples and Primitive Christians at the Pentecost, and such a change does, in fact, occur in the experience of all believers when they "have received the Holy Ghost *after* they have believed." Prior to this consummation, the vision of truth is dim, and the faith of the soul takes but a feeble hold of things unseen and eternal. As a consequence, the evidence of justification is obscure, and but small degrees of virtue proceed from Christ for moral and spiritual purification.

To do, or to endure, the soul has but very little strength; and with feeble and oft-slipping footsteps, it treads its weary way in the paths of obedience and of life. In such a twilight of Divine illumination there is hope; but doubt oftener predominates than assurance. There are, also, joys and consolations; but not "peace as a river, and righteousness as the waves of the sea." There is rather more of doubt than of hope, of fear than of assurance, and "an aching void within the soul," rather than "joy unspeakable and full of glory."

But when the Holy Ghost falls upon the believer, and his soul is "filled with the Spirit," in that baptism of fire, of love, of light, and joy in God, there is a cloudless apprehension of truth, and every truth apprehended has a transforming power upon the heart and character. The face of God, the love of Christ, "the glory of God and of the Lamb," are unveiled to the open vision of the mind. Hope dispels doubt, and assurance banishes fear. Weakness gives place to strength in God to do and to endure "all the good pleasure of His goodness, even the work of faith with power."

Instead of an aching void within, an infinite fulness of "living water springs up into everlasting life." In other words, there is in that day "a fountain opened to the house of David and to the inhabitants of Jerusalem for sin and for uncleanness."

Now it is to this higher form of experience, this outpouring of the Spirit promised to the Church in these latter days, that special reference is had in the text. You will observe that it is to "the house of David and to the inhabitants of Jerusalem"—that is, for believers within, and not for sinners without, the circle of the Church, that the fountain here referred to is to be opened.

In the context we read, that the time of the fulfillment of this prophecy is to be a period of great moral and spiritual power in the Church: "He that is feeble among them *at that day* shall be as David, and the house of David shall be as God, as the angel of the Lord before them." It is also to be a time of total moral and spiritual purification: "In that day there shall be upon the bells of the horses, *Holiness unto the Lord.*" Prior to that event, the instances of such high attainments would be few and far between. Then, this is to become the common experience of the Church universal.

This era of universal and total purification in the Church, this era of mighty power for the subjection of the world to the reign of Christ, is the theme of all the prophets, "when they testify beforehand of the sufferings of Christ, and of the glory that was to follow." St. John calls its introduction, "The marriage of the Lamb." "Let us be glad, and rejoice, and give honor to Him; for the marriage of the Lamb is come, and His wife hath made herself ready. And to her was granted to be clothed in fine linen, clean and white; for the fine linen is the righteousness of the saints." Referring to this era of Divine illumination, God, through the prophet Isaiah, thus addresses the Church: "Arise, shine; for thy light is come, and the glory of the Lord is risen upon thee. For, behold, the darkness shall cover the earth, and gross darkness the people: but the Lord shall arise upon thee, and His glory shall be seen upon thee. And the Gentiles shall come to thy light, and kings to the brightness of thy rising."

What a contrast in the state of the Church, as it has been in ages past, as it now is, and as it is to be in that day of light, and glory, and blessedness! Now, whatever of Divine glory she possesses is hardly recognized by the world, so feebly does her light shine. Then, that glory is to become visible and all-impressive to the world—so visible, and so impressive, that the race shall be drawn from the gross darkness with which they are encircled, to the light which is radiated from the face and throne of God upon the Church; just as the people were drawn from the darkness of Egypt to the light which illumined the Land of Goshen. And then this era of illumination is never to be eclipsed. "The Lord shall be thine everlasting light, and the days of thy mourning shall be ended."

In that day, according to the word of God through the prophet Jeremiah, God is to make a new covenant with His Church, and this is to be that covenant: "I will put My law in their inward parts, and write it in their hearts;" that is, sanctify them permanently and wholly. "Then," says God through the prophet Ezekiel, "will I sprinkle clean water upon you, and ye shall be clean; from all your filthiness and from all your idols will I cleanse you."

Of the *degree* of sanctification referred to in all these prophecies, we are distinctly informed in Jer. 1:20: "In those days, and at that time, saith the Lord, the iniquity of Israel shall be sought for, and there shall be none; and the sins of Judah, and they shall not be found." The prophet Joel refers to the same state of moral purification under the representation of a universal diffusion of the Holy Spirit upon the entire body of believers: "And it shall come to pass in the last days, saith God, I will pour out of My Spirit upon all flesh" [upon the entire company of believers], "and your sons and your daughters shall prophesy, and your young men shall see visions, and your old men shall dream dreams: and on My servants and on My handmaidens I will pour out in those days of My Spirit, and they shall prophesy."

No careful reader of the Scriptures can fail to perceive that the fountain referred to in the text is to be opened *within* the Church, and to and for believers as such; that they all, having "washed their garments, and made them white in the blood of the Lamb," may be, in Christ, "perfect and entire, wanting nothing." When the Church has thus attained, then will she become, in deed and in truth, a power in the world for its redemption. Ignorance and unbelief have hitherto kept the mass of believers straying in the wilderness with the flocks of Christ's foes. There their "follies have filled them with weeping."

In all ages, there have been a few who "have known and have believed the love of God to them," and thus knowing and believing, "their love has been made perfect." To the entire mass of believers, however, Christ is then to be "a fountain opened for sin and for uncleanness." In that day and at that time the love of all in common will be made perfect.

WHEN IS CHRIST SUCH A FOUNTAIN TO BELIEVERS?

The most important inquiry suggested by the text here presents itself—viz., By what means and under what circumstances will believers find in Christ this opened fountain? In other words, on what conditions does the grace of Christ, and the revelation of His glory and love, act upon the soul as an all-renovating power, emancipating it from "the bondage of corruption into the glorious liberty of the sons of God?"

We all know on what conditions and under what circumstances Christ becomes a fountain opened to the sinner for the pardon of sin. Through the power of the Spirit in connection with external and internal influences, he is led to think on his ways. In thus thinking, he distinctly apprehends the fact of his sin and of his hopeless ruin in sin. One want now presses upon him, and centers in itself the supreme desire of his soul—viz., pardon and acceptance with God. In this state he opens the Scriptures, and reads of Christ as the sinner's friend, the sinner's hope; or he meets with a Christian friend who points him to "the Lamb of God which taketh away the sin of the world."

The Spirit now so presents Christ to his sin-burdened soul that it apprehends in Him a present, immediate, and all-sufficient fulness for the overwhelming want with which it is burdened. Christ is now to that mind a fountain opened for sin; that is, for pardon, full and free. This convert meets some other sinner, and tells him of Christ as a Saviour from condemnation and the fear of death. That sinner, convinced of his own sin, and ruin in sin, beholds in Christ the needed redemption. Christ becomes to him, as in the former, a fountain opened for sin. Whenever the soul apprehends in Christ a present fulness for any pressing necessity, then He is to that mind "a fountain opened" for that want.

Now, when the soul has found in Christ "a fountain opened" for the forgiveness of sin, and when the joy and peace of its first love have passed away, it begins to feel the pressure of another want, more agonizing, if possible, than the first. It experiences an inward hunger and thirst for *another* blessing, more important even than pardon and the peace which the assurance of reconciliation with God can bring to the mind. It wants deliverance from "the bondage of corruption into the glorious liberty of the sons of God." It wants to be "pure in heart," that it may "see God." It wants to find in Christ, and in the gospel of His grace, a power not only for pardon, but for moral and spiritual renovation.

It reads in the Scriptures of an "eye-salve" by which we may see, and of an "anointing" by which we "know the things which are freely given us of God." It reads still further of Christ in the soul, "the hope of glory," and of God dwelling in us and walking in us, and thus becoming "our everlasting light," while the "days of our mourning are ended." It reads of a baptism of the Spirit—a baptism by which and in which "we all, beholding as in a glass the glory of the Lord, are changed into the same image from glory to glory," and are enabled to "comprehend the breadth, and length, and depth, and height, and to know the love of Christ, which passeth knowledge," and thus be "filled with all the fulness of God." In the midst of such revelations, and in the presence of such "exceeding great and precious promises," one desire possesses the whole powers of the soul—the desire to realize in its experience the fulness thus revealed to its faith and hope. Its one inquiry in great earnestness is, *How* and *where* can this fulness be obtained?

To receive an answer to this question, the individual sets about a most diligent and prayerful research. He makes inquiry of the most spiritual believers in the ministry and out of it, and reads the memoirs of such men as Brainerd and Payson. But all in vain. The Bible is a sealed book. In it he finds no present Christ addressed to the one present want of his whole being. "With strong crying and tears" he asks this single blessing of the Father in Heaven—that he "may know Him, and understand His way, and find grace in His sight;" that he may possess and be filled with the righteousness after which he now so inexpressibly hungers and thirsts, and be "endued with the power from on high," for which he is now waiting with such intense expectancy.

While thus praying, waiting, searching, hoping, and trusting, there is, through the Spirit, a direct manifestation of the glory, the love, the grace, and the fulness of Christ to his mind. In Christ he apprehends a present available and infinite fulness for every want of his immortal nature. The faith of his soul takes such a hold of the strength and fulness of Christ, as to become at once "strong in the Lord and in the power of His might," to do, to endure, to think, to feel, and to act for Christ. "All things have become new." Hope becomes changed into absolute assurance, and faith almost into a vision of things unseen and eternal. The veil is taken away from the Word of God. Its varied revelations of truths well out in "rivers of living water." Every truth realized has a quickening, vitalizing, and renovating power upon the mind. In other words, the believer, by a way which he knows not, now finds in Christ and in the gospel of His grace "a fountain opened for sin and for uncleanness."

Now this individual, thus, without learning, teaching, or external help, led to Christ, begins to speak to others of "the riches of the glory of this mystery," "which is Christ in you, the hope of glory." He speaks of Divine manifestations, of a "witness of the Spirit," of "a shedding abroad of the love of God in the heart," of a Divine indwelling in the soul, of a "fellowship with the Father, and with His Son Jesus Christ," of "everlasting consolations and good hope through grace," and of "joy unspeakable and full of glory," to all of which they are comparative strangers. Yet he speaks in a manner which renders them sensible of the fact, that "what he hath seen and heard, that he testifies." The hearing of such an experience awakens in them a thirst for these waters of life, and Christ, in this one mind, becomes to them "a fountain opened for sin and for uncleanness." God shines into one heart, and thus gives to all around "the light of the knowledge of the glory of God in the face of Jesus Christ."

So also when the membership of any one church becomes thus washed and purified, and made white "in the blood of the Lamb," Christ, in that church, becomes to all the churches and the world around, "a fountain opened for sin and for uncleanness." Thus streamlet intermingles with streamlet, till the waters of life, issuing from multitudes of sanctified hearts, become, in accordance with Ezekiel's vision, a mighty river that cannot "be passed over," and "the redeemed of the Lord return and come with singing unto Zion, and everlasting joy upon their heads; they obtain joy and gladness, and sorrow and sighing flee away."

You may now see, dear reader, when it is that you may regard yourself as standing upon the very banks of the river of life, where God is about to become the everlasting light of your soul. It is when, and only when, you have such a quenchless thirst for God, for holiness, and for the indwelling of the presence of Christ in your heart, that nothing else will satisfy you, or divert your thoughts or desire from this one infinite good, and when your whole being is centered in the immutable purpose to attain it. When the disciples were "all with one accord in one place," the set time had come when they were to be "endued with power from on high." Are you, reader, in a similar state? "Then lift up your head: your redemption draweth nigh!" But if you have no such purpose or desire, remember that you have no lot or part in this matter.

You also perceive when and how it is that Christ, in and through one individual, becomes to others "a fountain opened for sin and for uncleanness." It is not in the holding or the public advocacy of a form of doctrine or system of faith which accords with the truth that anyone occupies this Divine relation. It is, on the other hand, the holding and the advocacy of "the truth as it is in Jesus," and an inward experience and an outward life which accords with that truth. Were we an inquirer after the higher life in Christ, one of the last individuals that we would go to for light upon the subject, would be one who holds and advocates the doctrine of full redemption, and yet knows nothing of that truth as an all-vitalizing and renovating power. The most injurious influence that can exist in any church and community goes out from that person who zealously advocates that vital truth, and yet connects such advocacy with an unholy and corrupt life. The brightest jewel in Christ's crown of glory in any church, on the other hand, is the individual who holds and advocates that truth, and who has "received the Holy Ghost since he has believed." In him God dwells and walks, and Christ abides as an all-purifying, quickening, and life-imparting presence; and through him Christ and the provisions of His grace are perpetually revealed to the Church and the world around, as "a fountain opened for sin and for uncleanness"—the Divinest mission ever fulfilled by men or angels.

We also understand when it is that in any particular church Christ is revealed to other churches and the world around, as the fountain opened, of which we are speaking. That revelation is not made in and through the creed, or through the ministrations of the Church, however accordant both may be with the truth of God. There is no more unvitalizing power on earth than resides in a dead orthodoxy. To the sinner pressing the inquiry, "What must I do to be saved?" there is no spot where he is less likely to find the truth he seeks than in that place where the truth, and nothing but the truth, is held, advocated, and preached, and where that truth is belied and neutralized by a dead faith in the ministry and membership. To the inquirer after the higher life, there is no spot to him more dark than he finds in a church, and under a ministry, where this soul-renovating and heart-vitalizing truth is held, advocated, and preached, but where it exists in no hearts as "a well of water, springing up into everlasting life." The very truth itself then becomes to such a mind a mass of darkness, and nothing else, being presented as having no efficacy for moral and spiritual renovation. To the revelation under consideration, in and through any given church, two conditions must be fulfilled. The truth as it is in Jesus, in the first place, must be internally credited and openly advocated. It is "by the foolishness of preaching" that God saves those that believe. "Faith cometh by hearing." In the next place, the power, and renovating efficacy, and peace-giving and joy-imparting influence of the gospel, must be fully manifested in the inward experience and visible example of that church. Then, indeed, will that church be "a light in the world," and "have power with God and with men." Then, in and through such church, will Christ be to all encircling churches and to the world around, "a fountain opened for sin and for uncleanness." And when the churches of our God in general shall be similarly illuminated, "washed and made white in the blood of the Lamb," and all her membership are filled with the Spirit, and together "walk in the light of God," then will the Gentiles come to her light, and kings to the "brightness of her rising." In all the world, the spot where one such church is located will be the brightest, and, "to all who look for salvation in Israel," the most attractive, because that there the glory of Christ is revealed in this one Divine relation.

We may now clearly perceive what will hereafter constitute the glory or the shame of Methodism. The central article of her creed is the great central truth of the gospel, to wit: full and free redemption in Jesus Christ. In the holding and advocacy of that truth, her ministry and membership glory before the world. In her early founders and favorite memoirs, Christ and the promises of His grace are fully and distinctly revealed to all her membership and to all the world as "a fountain opened for sin and for uncleanness." Now, if this denomination shall remain true to her Heaven-descended mission, by continuing to hold and advocate this great truth, and by a living faith shall exemplify its all-purifying influence both before the Church and the world, this will be "her wisdom and her understanding," in the judgment of all nations, who shall hear of this great salvation. But if she should renounce faith in this great truth, or cease to advocate it, and above all, should hold it as a dead faith, instead of an all-vitalizing power, this would be her shame before God and the world. When in all the churches, in the sense explained, "there shall be a fountain opened for sin and for uncleanness" then is the millennium near, even at the door.

CHAPTER 12

The Consolation of the Spirit, or The Uses of Afflictive Providences

Take My yoke upon you, and learn of Me; for I am meek and lowly in heart: and ye shall find rest unto your souls.
—Matt. 11:29

I have refined thee, but not with silver; I have chosen thee in the furnace of affliction. —Isa. 48:19

THE FIGURE EXPLAINED

This one principle universally obtains in respect to the refinement of metals, that the severity of the process requisite to their purification is proportionate to their preciousness. No metal can be brought to a state of purity but by a trial of fire. Those of the least value can be melted and purified by comparatively small degrees of heat. Those of the highest value can be refined but by being placed in the central fires of the glowing furnace when heated to the greatest intensity. Silver *may* be placed in the furnace, but the heat of the common crucible is all that is requisite for its highest purification. The meaning of the text, then, is obvious. God says to the sanctified believer, this class being especially here addressed: "I have refined thee, but not with silver." "The virtues which I have purposed to develop in you being of all others the most precious and valuable in My estimation, I have subjected you to the action of the central fires of the furnace of affliction. Because I loved you, and saw in you a capacity to become possessed of the brightest and the best graces that adorn My kingdom, I placed you, for this purpose, in those central fires; and because you there lost all your tin and dross, and became the thing I desired, I chose you, when you were in that furnace, as My own peculiar treasure, and you shall 'be Mine in that day when I make up My jewels.'" There are some virtues which bloom up to maturity in circumstances of almost continued prosperity, and freedom from the pressure of strong temptation. Others, of a nobler birth, are matured and consolidated under the weight of great trusts and responsibilities. But those which take on the brightest possible forms of beauty and perfection are those which are refined and purified amid the glowing and melting heat of the furnace of affliction.

It is an immutable principle of the Divine government that all forms of real excellence shall be the result of *endurance* which severely tests and taxes the human faculties. A mind, for instance, stands before you, "with Atlanteon shoulders, fit to bear the weight of mightiest monarchies." How did that mind attain to such preeminence of power? It early began to think, to think *strongly,* and by long habit to the endurance of the weight of great thoughts, it towered up to its present overshadowing greatness. Endurance which brings such visible rewards men subject themselves to from choice. They delight to continue in it, because their nature is adapted to it, on the one hand, and on account of the "great recompense of reward" resulting from it on the other. The opposite in all respects obtains in regard to afflictive providences. They are objects of fear, and not of desire. They always come unsought, and descend upon the mind suddenly, as crushing avalanches from the heights above us. And what is still more peculiar in respect to them, is the fact that they are in themselves grievous burdens, with no visible or apparent benefits attending or issuing from them. Yet no events *appear* to come so directly from God as these. They seem to drop down upon us immediately from His hand, crushing our fondly-cherished hopes, smiting our persons till all our sensibilities quiver with excruciating agony, smiting also those most dear to us, and causing our hearts to bleed for sufferings we cannot relieve, and then taking from us even "the desire of our eyes with a stroke." These providences also most frequently, perhaps, strike that department of our nature most susceptible to suffering. How often do we hear individuals exclaim, "Anything but this! Why did God smite me in this one spot?" Yet, judging from appearance, God thus smites for no good reasons. What apparent good, for example, is there in that terrible bereavement by which the orphan is left, homeless and penniless, to the charity of this cold world? But, reader, it is amid the central fires of just such furnaces as these that the Divinest virtues known in the universe of God are refined and perfected; and those who are "made perfect through suffering" are the individuals who stand *nearest* the eternal throne in the kingdom of light.

This brings us to the subject of the present chapter—viz., the Divine uses of afflictive providences, acting, as they do, as disciplinary fires for the purification and perfection of the saints of God.

Before we proceed to a direct consideration of this subject, there is one thought to which very special attention is invited. Afflictive providences are in themselves, as above seen, crushing evils coming upon us for no visible reasons, and apparently tending to no good results. To *appearance* they are death-strokes falling upon our sensitive natures. Whether they shall issue in life or death to us, depends wholly upon the moral state in which they are received and endured. If, while we are in the crucible or in the furnace, "patience has her perfect work," we then become "perfect and entire, wanting nothing." If, in the same circumstances, the mind loses its spiritual balance, becomes chafed and fretted, restless and despondent; above all, if it loses hope and faith in God, then it loses its reward, and Satan takes its crown. In the history of the prophet Ezekiel we have a conspicuous example of a trial of faith successfully endured. God, through the prophet, desired to foreshadow to the nation the calamities which were impending—calamities so terrible, that even domestic bereavements, under their influence, would become matters of utter indifference; and God took this strange means to secure the result—to take suddenly from the prophet the wife of his youth, requiring him at the same time to move among the people as if no affliction had befallen him.

"Also the word of the Lord came to me, saying, Son of man, behold I take away from thee the desire of thy eyes with a stroke: yet neither shalt thou mourn nor weep, neither shall thy tears run down. Forbear to cry, make no mourning for the dead, bind the tire of thy head upon thee, and put on thy shoes upon thy feet, and cover not thy lips, and eat not the bread of men. So I spoke to the people in the morning: and at evening my wife died; and I did in the morning as I was commanded."

In every afflictive providence that befalls us, we are always distinctly addressed by duty in some specific form—more specific than in almost any other circumstances. Now it is when we do the specific thing then and there required of us, that we gain the virtues that ensure to us the crown of life. When racked with torturing pain, or smitten with domestic bereavement, we always hear in the depth of the soul the voice of God saying to us, "I have done this. Trust My will now, fully and distinctly; consent to suffer and endure, till I choose to remove the pain, or cease to bereave;" and we must "do as we are commanded." If loss of temporal good befalls, or temporal perplexities encircle us; if disappointments drop down upon us, or "hope deferred makes the heart sick"—then God again speaks within, saying to us, "Let your spirit now lie down and be still. Let no sentiment of discontent have place in your heart." Here, also, we must "do as we are commanded." When revilings, and falsehoods, and persecutions for righteousness' sake, encircle and descend upon us, the same voice within calls us from strife to prayer, from cursing to blessing, and from wrath to love. When reviled, we must bless; when defamed, we must entreat; and when persecuted, we must endure it, doing and enduring as we are commanded: "Hold fast *till* I come, and I will give thee a crown of life." Such is the command of the great Captain of our salvation. Holding fast, as required, we ensure the crown of life. Failing in this, we *miss* that crown.

We will now suppose that a believer has thus endured. *What will be the uses of such Divine providences in his experience?* This is the question to which a specific answer will now be attempted.

1. *Afflictions render things unseen and eternal real to the mind.* One of the most important of all these uses is the direct and immediate contact

into which the mind is then brought with God, duty, redemption, and immortality. Continued prosperity, abounding wealth, and freedom from pain and afflictive bereavements too often induce, not only a forgetfulness of God and of things unseen and eternal, but a proud denial of our accountability and dependence. When, on the other hand, afflictive providences come upon us, thought is suddenly arrested and fixed upon these objects of infinite concern. Under no other circumstances do they come so near, and give the mind such impressive opportunities and motives to adjust itself fully and rightly in respect to them. Philip of Macedon desired never to forget, in the midst of his superabounding prosperity, the fact of his own mortality. Hence he appointed a herald, whose exclusive mission was to repeat in the hearing of his sovereign, every time the latter left his palace, the words: "Philip, thou art mortal." Now, afflictive providences are Divine monitors, speaking to us with voices as from God out of Heaven, reminding us of God, duty, death, eternity, redemption, and retribution; and calling upon us to adjust the present, and future of our lives to these eternal verities. When mind has thus adjusted itself then these truths have a power over the thoughts, feelings, mental and moral activities, such as they could not otherwise acquire. As a consequence, they have corresponding power to refine, purify, and bless the soul, and fully prepare it to receive those "everlasting consolations" and immortal hopes with which God is ready to fill the utmost capacities of our inner being, whenever the heart is prepared to receive them. How many individuals have occasion to say with the psalmist, "It is good for me that I have been afflicted: for before I was afflicted I went astray. But now I have learned to keep Thy precepts." Thus it is that even in our afflictions "God dealeth with us a with sons," first teaching us the lesson of obedience, and then drawing us close, very close, to the bosom of His love.

2. *They discipline the human into subjection to the Divine will.* We are all aware, also, that the highest purity and blessedness of the soul depend mainly upon the right adjustment of the will of the creature relatively to the will of God. Now, afflictive providences bring the human into a more direct, immediate, and impressive contact with the Divine will, than any other. *Here* let the creature learn obedience, *here* "let patience

have her perfect work," and he "becomes perfect and entire, wanting nothing." He that walks with God amid the consuming heat of the glowing furnace, and there fully consents to endure and to suffer all the will of God: he that finds amid these central fires deep content, as his spirit lies down in the center of God's will, and is still—attains to a *disciplined* consolidation in Christian virtue, which renders his acquiescence in the Divine will, in all other relations, absolute. The soul now is permanently at peace with God, and, as a consequence, is fully prepared to be kept as permanently by "the peace of God, which passeth all understanding." Christian brethren, have you never had such a hallowed form of experience as this?—A dark and impenetrable cloud came over you and completely shut you in. You could not penetrate to the brightness which radiated from the upper surface of the cloud where all is turned towards the face of God. In the midst of the deep midnight around you, you dropped down into the center of the Divine will.

Let me suffer now your heart exclaims, let me suffer here, and anywhere, till God is fully satisfied. In this stillness of deep acquiescence, the first thought that begins to make melody in the depths of the soul, perhaps, is this: a moving apprehension of the *sweet will of God.* The sweet will of God, you begin to repeat, the sweet will of God. Let all my allotments be as God wills. Then there comes gently over you a sense of infinite *security* in God. The darkness around you is "but the shadow of His wing," beneath which you feel yourself to be "almost sacred." God is "covering you with His feathers," while beneath His wing you are fixing your trust, and resting there with perfect "quietness and assurance forever." You know now, as you otherwise could not have known, that under the all-shadowing protection of your God, "no evil can befall you; neither can any plague come nigh your dwelling." Light begins to penetrate through the cloud above you, till the deep midnight around becomes itself "all light, and its essence love." The cloud above has become all luminous. Through it you seem to see the face of God smiling with love ineffable into the depths of your soul. You know now why God afflicted you; your perfection in virtue, and your consequent entrance into the hallowed precincts of that rest which "remains for the people of God." Such are the unvarying issues of afflictive providences when, under their pressure, we "do as we are commanded."

3. *They strengthen and confirm Christian virtue.* These providences, also, tend very peculiarly to *strengthen* and *confirm* the faith and hopeful trust of the soul in God. When our own power and resources visibly fail us, we naturally turn from self to power out of and above ourselves. When finite confidences fall from under us, we are almost irresistibly impelled to lean upon the infinite. Now, afflictive providences are those Divine jostlings of the soul by which it is continually reminded of the power above, where our strength and safety lie concealed. As a consequence, they pre-eminently tend to induce the fixed habit of trust and hope in God. Did days of darkness never come, fulness of bread might induce forgetfulness of the Giver, and of dependence upon Him. Conscious weakness and want, however, center and fix the faith and hope of the soul in the power and fulness of God, and the frequent exercise of those virtues confirm, settle, and strengthen the mind in the same, till faith and hope in God become continuously habitual in the inward experience. Now mark the result. Leaning upon the Infinite, the soul becomes "strong in the Lord, and in the power of His might." Trusting in the Divine fulness, it receives of that fulness to the full measure of its conscious necessities. Hoping in God, hope deferred does not make the heart sick, and that "because the love of God is shed abroad in the heart by the Holy Ghost which is given unto us." As hope and trust in Christ become the fixed habit of the soul, in all our necessities the angel of His presence strengthens us, as the angel of God strengthened Him in the hour of His extremity. Everywhere, and under all circumstances, "the peace of God, which passeth all understanding, keeps our hearts and minds through Christ Jesus."

4. *They impart assurance of hope.* When the mind is put into the furnace of affliction, and learns obedience there, it attains, we remark, not only to a Divine purity and acceptance with God, but also, in the next place, to a more distinct *assurance* of its own gracious state, that it can hardly obtain in any other circumstances. Under no other circumstances, as we have seen, is the will of the creature brought into such direct and distinct contact with the will of God. Nowhere else, as a consequence, can

the mind be so distinctly conscious of absolute acquiescence in the Divine will, and subjection to it, as here: "Not as I will, but as Thou wilt." "The cup which my Father hath given me, shall I not drink it?" The character of such hallowed mental exercises as these cannot be misapprehended. Hence it is that, in the exercise of the same the mind has an absolute consciousness of its own gracious state, and of its consequent acceptance with God. Now this absolute assurance of the genuineness of our faith necessarily issues in corresponding assurance of hope: "And when tribulation has worked patience [confirmation in Christian virtue]: and patience, experience [assurance of our own gracious state]; and experience, hope," God never fails to lift upon the soul "the light of His countenance." "Hope," we repeat, "maketh not ashamed, because the love of God is shed abroad in the heart by the Holy Ghost which is given unto us." That state of meek, mild, and quiet submission which the patient endurance of suffering induces, fully prepares the mind to receive and appreciate God's *manifested* sympathy and love. The Holy Spirit now makes the soul distinctly conscious that "in all our afflictions God is afflicted, while the angel of His presence saves us," and we know, as we otherwise could not have known, how deeply God sympathizes with us and loves us. The light of God in which we now live and walk, sanctifies even the furnace through which we have been conducted, into this state of perpetual quietness and assurance, where "the days of our mourning are ended."

5. *They impart blessed visions of the eternal future.* There are also certain visions of the eternal future and of other kindred truths which nothing but the patient endurance of afflictive providences can prepare the mind to receive, and which the Holy Spirit never fails to impart when "patience has had her perfect work." Take the following as examples:—

"These light afflictions, which are but for a moment, work out for us a far more exceeding and eternal weight of glory." "All things work together for good to them that love God." "And God shall wipe away all tears from their eyes, and there shall be no more death, neither sorrow, nor crying, neither shall there be any more pain." "They shall hunger no more, neither thirst any more; neither shall the sun light on them, nor any heat. For the Lamb which is in the midst of the throne shall feed them, and shall lead them unto fountains of living waters." "Who shall separate us from the love of Christ? Shall tribulation, or distress, or persecution, or famine, or nakedness, or peril, or sword?" "Nay, in all *these* things we are more than conquerors through Him that loved us. For I am persuaded that neither death, nor life, nor angels, nor principalities, nor powers, nor things present, nor things to come, nor height, nor depth, nor any other creature, shall be able to separate us from the love of God which is in Jesus Christ our Lord." It is only as the mind passes through great tribulation, and becomes refined and purified in the midst of the same, that it can *fully* apprehend and appreciate the truths contained in such revelations as these; revelations which, when received, impart a fulness of joy otherwise impossible to us. Whatever our condition may be, let the Holy Spirit but open upon the mind such visions of the soul's eternal future, and render them conscious realities to its apprehension, and "the days of its mourning are ended." It is thus in genuine Christian experience that our most enduring joys well out from our deepest sorrows, and our most abiding consolations descend to us in the midst of our greatest tribulations, while the brightest hopes that gladden our hearts are "born, like the rainbow, in tears."

6. *They impart soul-satisfying visions of Christ.* As your heart has been pressed down under the weight of some great sorrow, did the Holy Spirit never open upon your spiritual vision an apprehension of Christ as a world-sufferer, of Christ in Gethsemane, in the judgment-hall, or upon the cross? In the presence of such a revelation, suffering and sorrow lose all power to distract the mind. On the other hand, they become sanctified in the mind's apprehension, and to "fill out the measure of Christ's sufferings" seems a privilege; and when sorrow for Christ's sake becomes a hallowed thing in the mind's regard, how infinite does the joy of the soul in Christ become! Thus, as in our deepest humiliation we find ourselves furthest within the precincts of Heaven, so in our greatest sufferings and sorrows do we behold most distinctly the face of God. In the furnace—strange kind of life that!—"we walk in the light of God."

7. *They develop the Divinest virtues in their Divinest forms.* We must not fail here to refer to the character of the Divine virtues which are

refined and perfected in the furnace of affliction. Nowhere else in the universe of God do we find such things of beauty as they. That meek submission, that subdued quietude of heart, that sweet and prompt turning of the soul to every indication of the Divine will, that tender sympathy with suffering in others, and readiness "to heal the broken-hearted," that deep and fixed trust in God, that serenity of hope, that crucifixion to the world, that mild purity of thought and life, and, above all, that fixed devotion to Christ; all these, blended in unison, render character a thing of beauty and perfection that even God loves to look at. Now, when the mind comes into this state it is then fully prepared to receive that fulness of joy for which God has been refining and perfecting it. In entering into this state the leading sentiment which pervades its whole inner being is what seems to be a feeling of infinite quietude and assurance. Then thoughts of ineffable consolation begin to drop down into the soul. Soon "visions of glory infinite come and go." At length the Sun of Righteousness rises upon the soul "with healing in His wings." In the everlasting light of that Sun, which continuously comes nearer and nearer to the soul, it moves onward, wondering with unutterable wonder that God should thus deign to shine upon a worm of the dust. God comes to dwell in the soul, and to walk in it, and make His abode there.

8. *They teach the soul what sorrow and affliction mean.* In such experiences the soul comes to learn, at length, what sorrow and affliction mean. They even become things of beauty to the mind. "We glory in tribulations also; knowing that tribulation worketh patience; and patience experience; and experience hope; and hope maketh not ashamed; because the love of God is shed abroad in our hearts by the Holy Ghost which is given unto us."

9. *They impart power for good to the Christian.* Nor are the Divine uses of afflictive providences confined to the subject who suffers. They fit him, as he otherwise could not be, to comfort them who are in any trouble, by the "comfort wherewith he is comforted of God." And never has the religion of Christ such power over worldly minds as when it is seen turning earth-born sorrows into Heaven-born joys.

Do you ask me, reader, when it is that you may regard patience as having had its perfect work in your experience? We answer, when you are deeply conscious that your will is so perfectly identified with the will of God, that you have no wish to possess any more of earthly good than God has appointed you, nor to diminish one jot or tittle of the full amount of affliction which He has allotted you. For myself, I should regard it as greatly criminal in me to entertain for a moment the wish that one throb of pain, one disappointed hope, a single bereavement, a single external affliction, that God appointed me, should fail to become real in my future of life, or to accomplish its Divine mission in my experience.

We now understand the light in which we should regard ourselves when causes of great sorrow fall upon us. First of all, we should carefully inquire whether these providences have come down from God out of Heaven, as *judgments* for wrongdoing, or as merely disciplinary trials of faith, and seek unto God accordingly. In neither case should we lose heart, or hope, or faith in God. We should conclude, at once, on the other hand, whatever the immediate cause or occasion of our sufferings may be, that God sees in us something which He desires to refine and perfect into a thing of beauty and perfection, for His own glory and ours, too; that He sees in us undeveloped capacities for good—capacities which He desires to perfect for the reception of those great and eternally enduring joys which He has prepared for us. Why should we be afraid of causes of sorrow, when, if we hold fast our integrity and faith in God, they are only the birth-throes of everlasting consolations, and deep and ever-enduring joys otherwise impossible to us.

We also now understand how a truly sanctified mind—one fully disciplined in "the furnace of affliction"—comes at length to regard such providences. To such minds they are "clouds of glory, coming from God who is our home"—clouds of glory, tinged all around their surfaces with light ineffable, and spreading over us the shadow of God's wing, beneath which, as we have said, we feel ourselves almost sacred. As light breaks through the cloud, and sweet and melting thoughts begin to gladden the heart, and heavenly consolations one after another drop down into the depths of the inner being; as the light of the Divine countenance is lifted up, and the sympathizing, loving smile of God becomes the feast of the soul—it exclaims, "Lord, it is good to be here!" and if God should so will, it would build its tabernacle and make its abode in this consecrated spot.

Perhaps some of my readers may be inclined to think that in the present chapter the picture has been overdrawn; that what has been presented never has been, and never can be, realized in actual experience. To test the question, let us go back, for a few moments, some eighteen hundred years, and speak with Paul upon the subject. You see him yonder, as he sits resting for an hour. He sits there in his chain, by the side of the soldier who keeps him. Let us approach him. How pale, and wan, and weary he looks! and yet what a halo of deep and abiding joy beams from his countenance and encircles his brow! Permit me to address him in your behalf. "Paul, we have heard much of that wonderful life and experience of yours, and have come to converse personally with you upon the subject. Will you impart to us the information we desire?" "With all my heart. But where shall I begin?" "Tell us first about your sufferings." "Well, I think that God hath set forth us, the apostles, last, as it were *appointed* unto death; for we are made a spectacle unto the world, and to angels, and unto men. *Even* unto this present hour we both hunger, and thirst, and are naked, and are buffeted, and have no certain dwelling place. We are made as the filth of the world, and are the offscouring of all things unto this day. But among the many who, in common with our Divine Lord, have been made perfect through suffering, I have been in labors more abundant, in stripes above measure, in prisons more frequent, in death oft. Of the Jews five times received I forty stripes, save one. Thrice was I beaten with rods; once was I stoned; thrice I suffered shipwreck; a night and a day have I been in the deep; in journeyings often, in perils of waters, in perils of robbers, in perils of mine own countrymen, in perils by the heathen, in perils in the city, in perils in the wilderness, in perils in the sea, in perils among false brethren; in weariness and painfulness, in watchings often, in hunger and thirst, in fastings often, in cold and nakedness. Besides those things which are without, that which cometh upon me daily—the care of all the churches. Who is weak, and I am not weak? Who is offended and I burn not?" "But, Paul, what has been your state of mind in the midst of these sufferings?" "As sorrowful, yet *always* rejoicing; as poor, yet making many rich; as having nothing, yet possessing all things. I have learned, in whatsoever state I am therewith to be content. I know both how to be abased, and I know how to abound: everywhere and in all things I am instructed both to be full and to be hungry, both to abound and to suffer need. I can do all things through Christ which strengtheneth me."

"But when you see that 'the foxes have holes, and the birds of the air have nests,' and in common with your Divine Master, you 'have not where to lay your head;' when you see other men dwelling in princely mansions, clad in costly array, and faring sumptuously every day; do you not *sometimes,* to say the least, envy their better lot, and feel dissatisfied with your own?" "I have coveted no man's silver, or gold, or apparel." "But when you go abroad with the distinct apprehension 'that bonds and afflictions abide you,' does not your sensitive nature *sometimes* shrink from the vision of the sufferings in prospect?" "None of these things move me, neither count I my life dear unto myself, so that I might finish my course with joy, and the ministry which I have received of the Lord Jesus, to testify the gospel of the grace of God."

Please answer this question also: "How do you now regard suffering for Christ's sake?" "I take pleasure in infirmities, in reproaches, in necessities, in persecutions, in distresses, for Christ's sake; for 'when I am weak then am I strong.'" "How did you attain to this blessed state?" "By simple faith in God. 'We believe, and therefore speak.'" "'I am crucified with Christ, nevertheless I live; yet not I, but Christ liveth in me; and the life which I now live in the flesh, I live by the faith of the Son of God, who loved me, and gave Himself for me.'"

Tell us this also, Paul. "May *we* thus attain?" "Most assuredly. 'He is able to save unto the *uttermost all* that come unto God by Him.'" "Paul, you appear very weak and exhausted; would to God we could come to you, and let you rest your weary head upon our bosom!" "I have just had a season of deep repose upon the bosom of Christ. As I sat here a few hours ago, He came to me in spirit, and said, 'You are weary, very weary. Lay your head upon My bosom, and rest there.' That season of deep intercommunion and fellowship 'with the Father, and with His Son Jesus

Christ,' has left me in a strait betwixt two; and what I shall choose, I wot not, 'having a desire to depart and be with Christ, which is far better; nevertheless, to abide in the flesh is more needful for my brethren. And having this confidence, I know that I shall abide and continue with them all for their furtherance and joy of faith.' I am refreshed now, and must attend to the multitude of converts and inquirers whom you see yonder coming to me for instruction. Farewell."

This, reader, is the glorious gospel of the blessed God. This is what that gospel did for Paul, what it has done for me, and what it is able to do for you. "If thou canst believe, all things are possible to him that believeth."

Suffering and sorrow have no place in the kingdom of light. In Heaven there is no more pain, sorrow, sighing, sickness, or death; no disappointed hopes, nor any form of heart-sickness from hope deferred. The *conception* of suffering and sorrow, however, and the remembrance of the same, constitute one of the central elements of the blessedness and glory of that kingdom. All the saints there wear upon their heads and carry in their hands crowns and palms of victory—victory through the blood of the Lamb, and in "great fights of affliction." Separate from that state the remembrance of afflictive providences, and from Christ the idea of a suffering God for human redemption, and you deprive Heaven itself of more than one-half of its light. The vision of glory which intensifies the rapture of the celestial hosts is that of Christ manifested through the emblem of a "Lamb slain from the foundations of the earth." We would request the reader to consider carefully the following passage, as an illustration of the truth before us:—

"And I beheld, and lo! in the midst of the throne and of the four beasts, and in the midst of the elders stood a Lamb as it had been slain, having seven horns and seven eyes, which are the seven spirits of God sent forth into all the earth. And He came and took the book out of the right hand of Him that sat upon the throne. And when He had taken the book, the four beasts and four-and-twenty elders fell down before the Lamb, having every one of them harps, and golden vials full of odors, which are the prayers of saints. And they sung a new song, saying, Thou art worthy to take the book and to open the seals thereof; for Thou wast slain, and hast redeemed us to God by Thy blood out of every kindred, and tongue, and people, and nation; and hast made us unto our God kings and priests: and we shall reign on earth. And I beheld, and I heard the voice of many angels round about the throne, and the beast and the elders; and the number of them was ten thousand times ten thousand, and thousands of thousands, saying with a loud voice, Worthy is the Lamb that was slain to receive the power, and riches, and wisdom, and strength, and honor, and glory, and blessing. And every creature which is in Heaven, and on the earth, and under the earth, and such as are in the sea, and all that are in them, heard I saying, Blessing, and honor, and glory, and power be unto Him that sitteth upon the throne, and unto the Lamb forever and ever. And the four beasts said, Amen. And the four-and-twenty elders fell down and worshipped Him that liveth forever and ever."

ADMONITION

Hereafter, when days of darkness come, when pain afflicts, when bereavements melt and adversity chastens our hearts, when the floods purify and the furnace refines our spirits, and the weight of great sorrow presses us down upon the bosom of God, let the fixed language of our souls be, "Welcome, Cross of Christ! welcome everlasting life."

God's Provision of Power

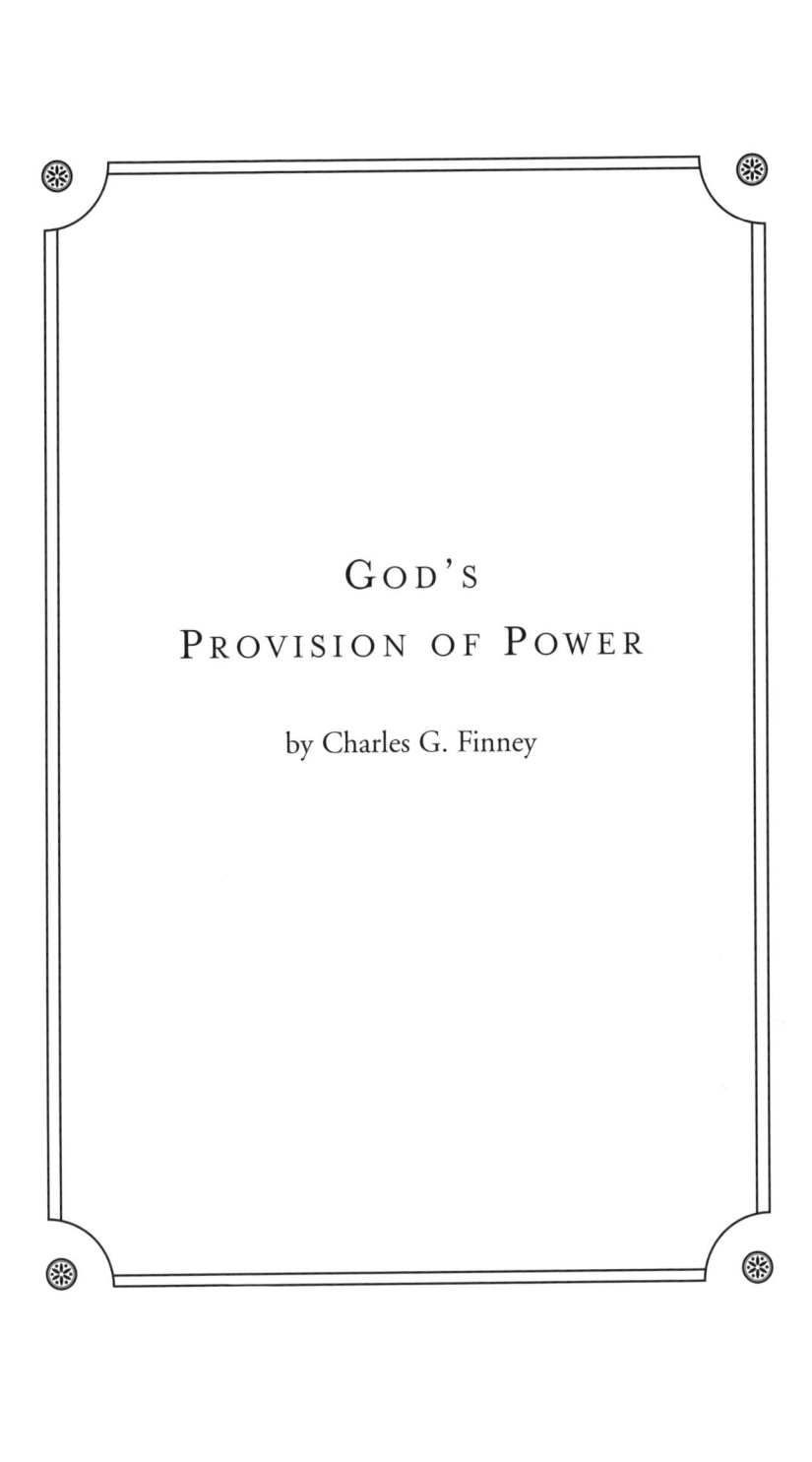

by Charles G. Finney

Chapter 1

Reasons Why the Power is Not Received

In my first remarks, I would call attention to the mission of the Church to disciple all nations, as recorded by Matthew and Luke, and state that this commission was given by Christ to the whole Church, and that every member of the Church is under obligation to make it his lifework to convert the world. Upon this I raise two inquiries: 1. What do we need to secure success in this great work? 2. How can we get it? *Answer:—*

1. We need the enduement of power from on high. Christ had previously informed the disciples that without Him they could do nothing. When He gave them the commission to convert the world, He added: "But tarry ye in Jerusalem till ye be endued with power from on high. Ye shall be baptized with the Holy Ghost not many days hence. Lo! I send upon you the promise of My Father." This baptism of the Holy Ghost, this blessing promised by the Father, this enduement of power from on high, Christ has expressly informed us, is the indispensable condition of performing the work which He has set before us.

2. How shall we get it?

• Christ expressly promised it to the whole Church, and to every individual whose duty it is to labor for the conversion of the world. He admonished the first disciples not to undertake the work *until* they had received this enduement of power from on high. Both the promise and the admonition apply equally to all Christians of every age and nation. No one has at any time any right to expect success unless he first secures the enduement of this power.

• The example of the first disciples teaches us how to secure this enduement. *They first consecrated themselves to the work, and continued in prayer and supplication until the Holy Ghost fell upon them, on the day of Pentecost, and they received the promised enduement of power from on high. This, then, is the way to get it.*

"If ye, then, being evil, know how to give good gifts unto your children, how much more shall your heavenly Father give the Holy Spirit to them that ask him." (Luke 11:13)

- This text informs us that it is delightfully easy to obtain the Holy Spirit, or this enduement of power, from the Father.
- That this is made a constant subject of prayer. Everybody prays for this, at all times; and yet, with all this intercession, how few, comparatively, are really endued with the Spirit of power from on high. This want is not met. The want of power is a subject of constant complaint. Christ says, "Everyone that asketh receiveth;" but there certainly is a "great gulf" between the asking and receiving, which is a serious stumbling block to many. How, then, is this discrepancy to be explained? The answer may appear in some one or all of the following statements:

1. We are not *willing,* upon the whole, to have what we desire and ask.
2. *God has expressly informed us that if we regard iniquity in ur hearts He will not hear us.* But the petitioner is often self-indulgent. This is iniquity, and God will not hear him.
3. He is uncharitable.
4. Censorious.
5. Self-dependent.
6. Resists conviction of sin.
7. Refuses to confess to all the parties concerned.
8. Refuses to make restitution to injured parties.
9. He is prejudiced and uncandid.
10. He is resentful.
11. He has a revengeful spirit.
12. Has a worldly ambition.
13. He has committed himself on some point, and become dishonest, and rejects further light.
14. He is denominationally selfish.

15. Selfish for his own congregation.
16. He resists the teaching of the Holy Spirit.
17. He grieves the Holy Spirit by dissension.
18. He quenches the Spirit by persistence in justifying wrong.
19. He grieves Him by a want of watchfulness.
20. He resists Him by indulging evil tempers.
21. Also by dishonesties in business.
22. Also by indolence and impatience in waiting upon the Lord.
23. By many forms of selfishness.
24. By negligence in business, in study, in prayer.
25. By undertaking too much business, too much study, and too little prayer.
26. By a want of entire consecration.
27. Last and greatest, by unbelief. He prays for this enduement without expecting to receive it. "He that believeth not God hath made Him a liar." This, then, is the greatest sin of all. What an insult, what a blasphemy, to accuse God of lying! I conclude by saying that these and other forms of indulged sin explain why so *little* is received, while so *much is asked.*

Someone may ask, "What is the other side?" The other side presents the certainty that we shall receive the promised enduement of power from on high, and be successful in winning souls, if we ask in faith and fulfill the plainly revealed conditions of prevailing prayer. "But if we first get rid of all the forms of sin which prevent our receiving this enduement, have we not already obtained the blessing? What more do we need?" *Answer:* There is a great difference between the *peace* and the *power* of the Holy Spirit in the soul. The disciples were Christians before the day of Pentecost, and as such had a measure of the Holy Spirit. They must have had the *peace* of sins forgiven, and of a justified state; but yet they had not the enduement of *power* necessary to the accomplishment of the work assigned them. They had the peace which Christ had given them, but not the power which He had promised. This may be true of all Christians; and right here is, I think, the great mistake of the Church and of the ministry. They rest in conversion, and do not seek until they obtain this enduement of power from on high. Hence, so many professors have no power with either God or man. They prevail with neither. They cling to a hope in Christ, and even enter the ministry, overlooking the admonition to wait until they are endued with power from on high. But let anyone bring all the tithes and offerings into God's treasury, let him lay all upon the altar, and prove God herewith, and he shall find that God "will open the windows of Heaven, and pour him out a blessing that there shall not be room enough to receive it."

CHAPTER 2

An Exhibition of the Power From on High

§

But ye shall receive power, after that the Holy Ghost is come upon you: and ye shall be witnesses unto Me both in Jerusalem, and in all Judaea, and in Samaria, and unto the uttermost part of the earth.
—Acts 1:8

In the present chapter I will relate an exhibition of this power from on high, as witnessed by myself. Soon after I was licensed to preach I went into a region of country where I was an entire stranger. I went there at the request of a Female Missionary Society, located in Oneida County, New York. Early in May, I think, I visited the town of Antwerp, in the northern part of Jefferson County. I stopped at the village hotel, and there learned that there were no religious meetings held in that town at the time. They had a brick meetinghouse, but it was locked up. By personal efforts I got a few people to assemble in the parlor of a Christian lady in the place, and preached to them on the evening after my arrival. As I passed around the village, I was shocked with the horrible profanity that I heard among the men wherever I went. I obtained leave to preach in the schoolhouse on the next Sabbath; but before the Sabbath arrived I was much discouraged, and almost terrified, in view of the state of society which I witnessed. On Saturday the Lord applied with power to my heart the following words, addressed by the Lord Jesus to Paul, Acts 18:9, 10: "Be not afraid, but speak, and hold not thy peace; for I am with thee, and no man shall set on thee to hurt thee; for I have much people in this city." This completely subdued my fears; but my heart was loaded with agony for the people.

On Sunday morning I arose early, and retired to a grove not far from the village to pour out my heart before God for a blessing on the labors of the day. I could not express the agony of my soul in words; but struggled, with much groaning and, I believe, with many tears, for an hour or two without getting relief. I returned to my room in the hotel; but almost immediately came back to the grove. This I did thrice. The last time I got complete relief, just as it was time to go to meeting.

I went to the schoolhouse, and found it filled to its utmost capacity. I took out my little pocket Bible, and read for my text: "God so loved the world, that He gave His only begotten Son, that whosoever believeth in Him should not perish, but have everlasting life." I exhibited the love of God in contrast with the terrible manner in which He was treated by those for whom He gave up His Son. I charged home their profanity upon them; and, as I recognized among my hearers several whose profanity I had particularly noticed, in the fulness of my heart and the gushing of my tears, I pointed to them, and said, "I heard these men call upon God to damn their fellows." The Word took powerful effect. Nobody seemed offended, but almost everybody greatly melted. At the close of the service, the amiable landlord, Mr. Copeland, rose and said that he would open the meeting-house in the afternoon. He did so. The meeting-house was full, and, as in the morning, the Word took powerful effect. Thus a powerful revival commenced in the village, which soon after spread in every direction.

I think it was on the second Sabbath after this, when I came out of the pulpit in the afternoon, an aged man approached, and said to me, "Can you not come and preach in our neighborhood? We have never had any religious meetings there." I inquired the direction and the distance, and appointed to preach there the next afternoon, Monday, at five o'clock, in their schoolhouse. I had preached three times in the village, and attended two prayer-meetings on the Lord's day; and on Monday I went on foot to fulfill this appointment. The weather was very warm that day, and before I arrived there I felt almost too faint to walk, and greatly discouraged in my mind. I sat down in the shade by the wayside, and felt as if I was too faint to reach there, and if I did, too much discouraged to open my mouth to the people.

When I arrived I found the house full, and immediately commenced the service by reading a hymn. They attempted to sing, but the horrible discord agonized me beyond expression. I leaned forward, put my elbows upon my knees and my hands over my ears, and shook my head withal, to shut out the discord, which even then I could barely endure. As soon as they had ceased to sing, I cast myself down upon my knees, almost in a state of desperation. The Lord opened the windows of Heaven upon me, and gave me great enlargement and power in prayer. Up to this moment I had had no idea what text I should use on the occasion. As I rose from my knees the Lord gave me this: "Up, get you out of this place, for the Lord will destroy this city." I told the people, as nearly as I could recollect, where they would find it, and went on to tell them of the destruction of Sodom. I gave them an outline of the history of Abraham and Lot, and their relations to each other; of Abraham's praying for Sodom; and of Lot as the only pious man that was found in the city.

While I was doing this I was struck with the fact that the people looked exceedingly angry about me. Many countenances appeared very threatening, and some of the men near me looked as if they were about to strike me. This I could not understand, as I was only giving them, with great liberty of spirit, some interesting sketches of Bible history. As soon as I had completed the historical sketch, I turned upon them, and said that I had understood they had never had any religious meetings in that neighborhood; and applying that fact, I thrust at them with the sword of the Spirit with all my might. From this moment the solemnity increased with great rapidity. In a few moments there seemed to fall upon the congregation an instantaneous shock. I cannot describe the sensation that I felt, nor that which was apparent to the congregation; but the Word seemed *literally* to cut like a sword.

The power from on high came down upon them in such a torrent that they fell from their seats in every direction. In less than a minute nearly the whole congregation were either down on their knees, or on their faces, or in *some* position prostrate before God. Everyone was crying or groaning for mercy upon his own soul. They paid no further attention to me or to my preaching. I tried to *get* their attention; but I could not. I observed the aged man who had invited me there, still retaining his seat near the center of the house. He was *staring* around him with a look of unutterable astonishment.

Pointing to him, I cried at the top of my voice: "Can't you *pray?*" He knelt down and roared out a short prayer, about as loud as he could halloo; but they paid no attention to him. After looking round for a few moments, I knelt down and put my hand on the head of a young man who was kneeling at my feet, and engaged in prayer for mercy on his soul. I got his attention, and preached Jesus in his ear. In a few moments he seized Jesus by faith, and then broke out in prayer for those around him. I then turned to another in the same way, and with the same result; and then another, and another, till I know not how many had laid hold of Christ and were full of prayer for others.

After continuing in this way till nearly sunset, I was obliged to commit the meeting to the charge of the old gentleman who had invited me, and go to fulfill an appointment in another place for the evening. In the afternoon of the next day I was sent for to go down to this place, as they had not been able to break up the meeting. They had been obliged to leave the school-house, to give place to the school; but had removed to a private house near by, where I found a number of persons still, too anxious and too much loaded down with conviction to go to their homes. These were soon subdued by the Word of God, and I believe all obtained a hope before they went home.

Observe, I was a total stranger in that place, had never seen nor heard of it until as I have related. But here, at my second visit, I learned that the place was called Sodom, by reason of its wickedness; and the old man who invited me was called Lot, because he was the only professor of religion in the place. After this manner the revival broke out in this neighborhood. I have not been in that neighborhood for many years; but in 1856, I think, while laboring in Syracuse, New York, I was introduced to a minister of Christ from the St. Lawrence County, by the name of Cross. He said to me: "Mr. Finney, you don't know me; but do you remember preaching in a place called Sodom?" &c. I said: "I shall never forget it." He replied: "I was then a young man, and was converted at that meeting." He is still living, a pastor in one of the churches in that county, and is the father of the principal of our preparatory department. Those who have lived in that region can testify of the permanent results of that blessed revival. I can only give in words a *feeble* description of that wonderful manifestation of power from on high attending the preaching of the Word.

Chapter 3

Who May Expect this Enduement of Power

If ye love me, keep My commandments. And I will pray the Father, and He shall give you another Comforter, that He may abide with you for ever; Even the Spirit of truth; whom the world cannot receive, because it seeth Him not, neither knoweth Him: but ye know Him; for He dwelleth with you, and shall be in you.
—John 14:15–17

I need not now give other instances of the manifestation of this "power from on high," since its existence is admitted, and has been witnessed in every age of the Church. The two instances given in the former chapter were exceptional in certain respects. But I could multiply to almost any extent accounts of instances of the manifestation of this power upon individuals and upon masses. This power has often been manifested in private conversation, in public exhortation, in public and social prayer, and in every manner of communicating truth. It is well understood that oftentimes an invisible but all-subduing power attends the communication of God's truth; and that the manifestation of this power is seen to accompany the labors of some individuals much more strikingly than it does those of others. If it would not try the patience of my readers, I should like to notice many illustrations of this remark, and name the persons who were manifestly endued with this power, and the places where such manifestations were made. But I pass to the consideration of the question: "Who have a right to expect this enduement of power to win souls to Christ?"

1. The command to disciple all nations was given to the whole Church, and not merely to the apostles. I believe this is generally admitted.

The injunction to tarry at Jerusalem until they received this enduement was also given to the then-existing Christian Church. The promise of this enduement appears to have been given to all whose duty it was to labor for the conversion of the world. The promise, as usual, was coextensive with the command.

2. The work to be done is many-sided, and a variety of gifts is essential to its accomplishment. These were richly bestowed by Christ on the day of Pentecost, and have been richly multiplied by Him in every age of the Church. But all other gifts are unavailing without the addition of this marvelous power to impress God's saving truth upon the soul. Are we to conclude that this power is a gift promised to and designed for only a select few; or was it promised as a gift common to all God's people? May they all be endued with this power from on high by fulfilling the conditions of its bestowment? This is a momentous question. For, if it is not promised to all, to whom is it promised? The promise is nugatory and void, for uncertainty, unless we can ascertain to whom it is made.

1. The promise certainly was not confined to the apostles, neither was the enduement confined to them; for in the apostolic age Stephen, with many others—and, indeed, the whole Church—possessed this power. Again, it was not then, nor has it been since, confined to ordained ministers of the gospel. It has always been possessed by laymen, and in many instances in an eminent degree. I have myself known a great many laymen who were marvelously gifted in winning souls to Christ. Who has not heard of Father Carpenter (mentioned by Dr. Mahan in another part of this volume) a layman, but little educated, and of quite limited natural ability? He labored in Southern New York and New Jersey as a layman; and hundreds—I think I may say thousands—were the seals of his labors. I could name scores of laymen whose exhortations and conversations have been instrumental in converting hundreds upon hundreds of souls.

This enduement was not at first, nor has it been since, confined to the male sex. Women have possessed it, and very often in a remarkable degree. Paul had his female helpers in proclaiming the gospel, whose usefulness he was frank to acknowledge. In every age of the Church, and especially wherever revivals of religion have existed, this power has been given to women as well as men. I am rejoiced to know that the American Board is learning more and more the power and usefulness of female labors in the missionary field. However men may interpret the Bible, whatever prejudices may exist in any branch of the Church against the public gospel labors of females, the fact remains that God imparts to females, often in an eminent degree, the power to win souls to Christ. I have myself known a goodly number of women who have been amongst the most efficient laborers for souls that I could anywhere find. I could name women of diverse ages and culture upon whom this power from on high rested in a degree too manifest to be overlooked or denied. This enduement, then, is not confined to either sex.

This power has been possessed by both young and old, by young converts, and by ripe Christians. Many have possessed it from their first conversion, whilst others have failed to obtain it until they had been in the Church for many years. I have known ministers, who had labored many years without it, at last come to possess it in an eminent degree. Facts undeniably prove that this enduement of power from on high is and has been a gift common to Christians of all ages and sexes, and of every degree of condition. So that all Christians, by virtue of their relation to Christ, may ask and receive this enduement of power to win souls to Him. It is evident that the promise was not originally made to any particular individuals, to the exclusion of others. It is also manifest that the bestowment of the gift has not been confined to office, age, or sex. So far as my observation has gone, I have found it to exist as frequently among laymen as clergymen, and nearly as often among women as men, and quite as often among young converts as older professors of religion. Were it necessary, I could summon a cloud of witnesses as proofs and illustrations of what I here assert.

I have said that Christians belonging to all classes possess this enduement of power savingly to impress the souls of men—young converts, old professors of religion, ministers, laymen, women, old and young, and of every degree of human culture. The history of the Church affords evidence that there has always been a sprinkling of Christians, of ministers, and laymen and women, that have been peculiarly gifted in winning souls to Christ. Now, I must not fail to add, and that with emphasis, that these persons have been without exception, especially anointed for this work.

After the first faith they have received the special enduement of power from on high. Men and women vary indefinitely in their natural powers of persuasion, but no human eloquence can ever convert a soul. Unless the Spirit of God sets home and makes the truth of God effectual, all human eloquence and learning will be in vain. And it is a fact worthy of all attention and consideration, that, with very little human culture, this enduement of power will make a Christian wise and efficient in bringing souls to Christ. The apostles, with the exception of Paul, had but little culture; and yet witness the effect of the fisherman Peter's first sermon, after receiving his first baptism of this power.

I have referred to Father Carpenter. Whoever was acquainted with him, and has known anything of the results of his labors, must have been astonished at his success, considering his very limited culture. It is very humiliating to human learning and pride, and always has been; nevertheless, it has been Christ's method from the first to choose the weak things of this world to confound the wise. I have said that this enduement of power is often given to females. The Church has greatly erred in keeping them back, and not encouraging them in personal efforts to win souls to Christ. From my own experience and observation I am convinced that, were they encouraged by conversation, exhortation, persuasion, and every suitable method to make efforts to win souls, it would be found that there is in the Church a great host of women endued with this power.

This enduement of power is sometimes bestowed immediately after conversion. It was in my own case. I possessed it from the very first as fully as I have done in any period of my life. It is not a thing into which people can gradually grow by forming habits of persuasion and conversation. It is a gift—an anointing, instantaneously received, and that may be enlarged or diminished as the possessor of it uses it more or less faithfully and intensely for the purposes for which it was given. It is oftentimes possessed and then lost, or its manifestation suspended by something that quenches the light of the Spirit in the soul. I have myself seen striking examples of this.

I have said that this power often rests upon those who have very little human culture. This is a notorious fact; but it does not follow from this that culture is to be despised or to be little accounted of. Where this power exists, the more learning and eloquence the better. But it is painful to observe the constant tendency to substitute culture for this power, or human learning and eloquence in place of this Divine enduement. I fear this tendency is increasing in the Church. The churches are calling for men of great learning and eloquence, instead of men who are deeply baptized with the Holy Ghost.

The seminaries of learning are much in fault in this thing. They do not lay half stress enough upon the possession of this enduement as an essential qualification for usefulness in the world. The manifest possession of this enduement of power should be considered an indispensable qualification for a professor in college or in a theological seminary, and the want of it should be regarded as a disqualification for a professorship, especially in a theological seminary. A theological professor who does not believe in this enduement of power, and who does not possess it in a manifest degree, cannot fail to be a stumbling block to his students. If he does not urge it upon them as the most important of all qualifications for the ministry, if he does not speak of it and treat it as altogether indispensable to success in the ministry, his teaching and his influence will be vitally defective; they will be a snare and a stumbling block. This must be true, or this whole question of the enduement of power from on high must be a delusion. This enduement is nothing, or it is everything in the sense of being wholly indispensable to success. It is a notorious fact and no delusion; and the want of it should be regarded by the churches as a disqualification for the pastoral office, or for superintendent of the Sabbath School, or for deacons or elders of the church, or for home or foreign missionaries. Pastors should urge the necessity of this enduement upon their churches, and raise up helpers in the gospel, and surround themselves with a host of men and women who are richly endued with power from on high. If a pastor has to work alone, if he has no members, or but a few, who are endued with this power, it is generally because he does not possess it himself; or, if he does possess it, he fails in so presenting and urging it as to procure its acceptance by the members of his church.

CHAPTER 4

The Conditions of Receiving this Power

§

And, behold, I send the promise of My Father upon you: but tarry ye in the city of Jerusalem, until ye be endued with power from on high.—Luke 24:49

In this chapter I propose to consider the conditions upon which this enduement of power can be obtained. Let us borrow a light from the Scriptures. I will not cumber this chapter with quotations from the Bible, but simply state a few facts that will readily be recognized by all readers of the Scriptures. If the reader will read in the last chapter of Matthew and of Luke the commission which Christ gave to His disciples, and in connection read the first and second chapters of the Acts of the Apostles, he will be prepared to appreciate what I have to say.

1. The disciples had already been converted to Christ, and their faith had been confirmed by His resurrection. But here let me say that conversion to Christ is not to be confounded with a consecration to the great work of the world's conversion. In conversion the soul has to do directly and personally with Christ. It yields up its prejudices, its antagonisms, its self-righteousness, its unbelief, its selfishness; accepts Him, trusts Him, and supremely loves Him. All this the disciples had, more or less, distinctly done. But as yet they had received no definite commission, and no particular enduement of power to fulfill a commission.

2. But when Christ had dispelled their great bewilderment resulting from His crucifixion and confirmed their faith by repeated interviews with them, He gave them their great commission to win all nations to Himself. But He admonished them to tarry at Jerusalem till they were

endued with power from on high, which He said they should receive not many days hence. Now observe what they did. They assembled—the men and women—for prayer. They accepted the commission, and, doubtless, came to a mutual understanding of the *nature* of the commission, and the necessity of the spiritual enduement which Christ had promised. As they continued day after day in prayer and conference, they, no doubt, came to appreciate more and more the difficulties that would beset them, and to feel more and more their inadequacy to the task. A consideration of the circumstances and results leads to the conclusion that they one and all consecrated themselves, with all they had, to the conversion of the world as their life-work. They must have renounced utterly the idea of living to themselves in any form, and devoted themselves with all their powers to the work set before them. This consecration of themselves to the work, *this self-renunciation, this dying* to all that the world could offer them, must, in the order of nature, have preceded their intelligent seeking of the promised enduement of power from on high. They then continued, with one accord, in prayer for the promised baptism of the Spirit, which baptism included all that was essential to their success.

Observe, they had a work set before them. They had a promise of power to perform it. They were admonished to wait until the promise was fulfilled. *How* did they wait? Not in listlessness and inactivity; not in making preparations, by study and otherwise, to get along without it; not by going about their business, and offering an occasional prayer that the promise might be fulfilled; but they *continued* in prayer, and persisted in their suit till the answer came. They understood that it was to be a baptism by the Holy Ghost. They understood that it was to be received from Christ. They prayed in faith. They held on, with the firmest expectations, until the enduement came. Now, let these facts instruct us as to the conditions of receiving this enduement of power.

We, as Christians, have the same commission to fulfill. As truly as they did we need an enduement of power from on high. Of course, the same injunction, to wait upon God till we receive it, is given to us.

We have the same promise that they had. Now, let us take substantially and in spirit the same course that they did. They were Christians, and had a measure of the Spirit to lead them in prayer and in consecration. So have we. Every Christian possesses a measure of the Spirit of Christ; enough of the Holy Spirit to lead us to true consecration, and inspire us with the faith that is essential to our prevalence in prayer. Let us, then, not grieve or resist Him; but accept the commission, fully consecrate ourselves, with all we have, to the saving of souls as our great and our only life-work. Let us get onto the altar with *ALL* we have and are, and lie there and persist in prayer till we receive the enduement. Now, observe, conversion to Christ is not to be confounded with the acceptance of this commission to convert the world. The first is a personal transaction between the soul and Christ, relating to its own salvation. The second is the soul's acceptance of the service in which Christ purposes to employ it. Christ does not require us to make brick without straw. To whom He gives the commission He also gives the admonition and the promise. If the commission is heartily accepted, if the promise is believed, if the admonition to wait upon the Lord till our strength is renewed be complied with, we shall receive the enduement.

It is of the last importance that all Christians should understand that this commission to convert the world is given to them by Christ individually.

Everyone has the great responsibility devolved upon him or her to win as many souls as possible to Christ. This is the great privilege and the great duty of all the disciples of Christ. There are a great many departments in this work. But in every department we may and ought to possess this power; that whether we preach, or pray, or write, or print, or trade, or travel, take care of children, or administer the government of the state, or whatever we do, our whole life and influence should be permeated with this power. Christ says: "If any man believe in Me, out of his belly shall flow rivers of living water"—that is, a Christian influence, having in it the element of power to impress the truth of Christ upon the hearts of men, shall proceed from him. The great want of the Church at present is, first, the realizing conviction that this commission to convert the world is given to each of Christ's disciples as His life-work. I fear I must say that the great mass of professing Christians seem never to have been impressed with this truth. The work of saving souls they leave to ministers.

The second great want is a realizing conviction of the necessity of this enduement of power upon every individual soul. Many professors of religion suppose it belongs especially and only to such as are called to preach the gospel as a life-work. They fail to realize that all are called to preach the gospel; that the whole life of every Christian is to be a proclamation of the glad tidings.

A third want is an earnest faith in the promise of this enduement. A vast many professors of religion, and even ministers, seem to doubt whether this promise is to the whole Church and to every Christian. Consequently they have no faith to lay hold of it. If it does not belong to all, they don't know to whom it does belong. Of course they cannot lay hold of the promise by faith.

A fourth want is that persistence in waiting upon God for it that is enjoined in the Scriptures. They faint before they have prevailed, and, hence, the enduement is not received. Multitudes seem to satisfy themselves with a hope of eternal life for themselves. They never get ready to dismiss the question of their own salvation; leaving that, as settled, with Christ. They don't get ready to accept the great commission to work for the salvation of others, because their faith is so weak that they do not steadily leave the question of their own salvation in the hands of Christ; and even some ministers of the gospel, I find, are in the same condition, and halting in the same way, unable to give themselves wholly to the work of saving others, because in a measure unsettled about their own salvation. It is amazing to witness the extent to which the Church has practically lost sight of the necessity of this enduement of power! Much is said of our dependence upon the Holy Spirit by almost everybody; but how little is this dependence realized. Christians, and even ministers, go to work without it. I mourn to be obliged to say that the ranks of the ministry seem to be filling up with those who do not possess it. May the Lord have mercy upon us! Will this last remark be thought uncharitable? If so, let the report of the Home Missionary Society, for example, be heard upon this subject. Surely, something is wrong.

An average of five souls won to Christ by each missionary of that society in a year's toil certainly indicates a most alarming weakness in the ministry. Have all, or even a majority of these ministers, been endued with the power which Christ promised? If not, why not? But, if they have, is this all that Christ intended by His promise? In a former chapter I have said that the reception of this enduement of power is instantaneous. I do not mean to assert that in every instance the recipient was aware of the precise time at which the power commenced to work mightily within him. It may have commenced like the dew, and increased to a shower. I have alluded to the report of the Home Missionary Society. Not that I suppose that the brethren employed by that society are exceptionally weak in faith and power as laborers for God. On the contrary, from my acquaintance with some of them, I regard them as among our most devoted and self-denying laborers in the cause of God. This fact illustrates the alarming weakness that pervades every branch of the Church, both clergy and laity. Are we not weak? Are we not criminally weak? It has been suggested that by writing thus I should offend the ministry and the Church. I cannot believe that the statement of so palpable a fact will be regarded as an offense. The fact is, there is something sadly defective in the education of the ministry and of the Church. The ministry is weak because the Church is weak. And then, again, the Church is kept weak by the weakness of the ministry. Oh! for a conviction of the necessity of this enduement of power and faith in the promise of Christ.

Bless your friends and family with *The Baptism of the Holy Spirit/ God's Provision of Power* for $10.99 each!

Order Form

_____ Yes, I want _____ copies of *The Baptism of the Holy Spirit/ God's Provision of Power* at $10.99 each.

Include $3.95 shipping for one book, and $1.95 for each additional book. New York residents must include 8% sales tax. Canadian orders please include $10.99 plus $4.95 shipping for one book, and $2.95 for each additional book, in US funds, with 7% GST added.

Payment must accompany orders. Orders ship in 48 hours.

My check or money order for $ _____ is enclosed.

Name _____
Organization _____
Address _____
City _____ State _____ Zip _____
Phone _____ E-mail _____

Make your check payable and return to:

Williams Publishers
3843 Fountain St.
Clinton, NY 13323
315.853.4217